CoronaDef Workshop 2021

AA005227

Online
21 February 2021

ISBN: 978-1-7138-3763-3

Printed from e-media with permission by:

Curran Associates, Inc.
57 Morehouse Lane
Red Hook, NY 12571

Some format issues inherent in the e-media version may also appear in this print version.

The Internet Society
11710 Plaza America Drive, Suite 400
Reston, VA 20190
U.S.A.

Phone: (703) 439-2120
Fax: (703) 326-9881

www.internetsociety.org

Additional copies of this publication are available from:

Curran Associates, Inc.
57 Morehouse Lane
Red Hook, NY 12571 USA
Phone: 845-758-0400
Fax: 845-758-2633
Email: curran@proceedings.com
Web: www.proceedings.com

Table of Contents

Proceedings

CoronaDef 2021

Innovative Secure IT Technologies against COVID-19 (CoronaDef) Workshop

February 21, 2021
Virtual

Hosted by the

Internet Society

Internet Society
11710 Plaza America Drive
Suite 400
Reston, VA 20190

Address your correspondence to: NDSS Program Manager, Internet Society, 11710 Plaza America Drive, Suite 400, Reston, VA 20190 USA, tel. +1 703 439 2120, fax +1 703 326 9881, ndss@elists.isoc.org.

The papers included here comprise the proceedings of the meeting mentioned on the cover and title page. They reflect the authors' opinions and, in the interest of timely dissemination, are published as presented and without change. Their inclusion in this publication does not necessarily constitute endorsement by the editors or the Internet Society.

Internet Society
11710 Plaza America Drive
Suite 400
Reston, VA 20190
tel +1 703.439.2120
fax +1 703.326.9881
http://www.internetsociety.org

Message from the Program Co-Chairs

It is our great pleasure to welcome you to the CoronaDef Workshop. This workshop is organized to contribute to new and innovative secure technologies against COVID-19. The current worldwide spread of the COVID-19 pandemic confronts human societies with entirely new challenges that have not existed in this form in the digital age. Strategies to combat the spread of the pathogen are therefore largely based on "traditional" measures such as behavioral recommendations, restrictions to free movement of persons, the shutdown of schools, organizations and companies, and the identification and quarantine of infected people based on medical testing. Modern digital technologies provide promising opportunities to complement the above-mentioned measures and increase their effectiveness, e.g., by enabling quarantine measures to target potentially infected people faster and in a more focused manner. Indeed, due to the current quarantine situation, the Internet and its services constitute "the" information gateway for many societies. Digital technologies can aid the vaccination in terms of providing information systems for managing vaccination processes, vaccination passports as well as logistical and tracking services. However, these technologies are faced with a variety of security and privacy challenges which they need to tackle to build trust and acceptance in our societies.

In response to the call for papers of CoronaDef, 10 papers were submitted. Each paper received at least three reviews. The program committee selected seven papers to be presented at the Workshop. These papers cover a different topic, ranging from contact tracing techniques to cybersecurity tools to allow small businesses to assess their online workflows. The workshop includes two expert keynote speakers who provide their view on the security and privacy problems of contact tracing schemes as well as on experiences in supporting FEMA/HHS COVID task force. The workshop closes with an expert panel on various challenges to encounter in fighting the pandemic.

The organization of a workshop requires the collaboration of many individuals. First, we would like to thank the authors for submitting to the Workshop. Second, we thank the program committee members for their efforts in reviewing the papers and providing valuable feedback to authors.

We hope that you will find this program interesting and that the Workshop will provide you with a valuable opportunity to interact with other researchers and practitioners in this field.

Ahmad-Reza Sadeghi
TU Darmstadt

Farinaz Koushanfar
UCSD

Trent Jaeger
Pennsylvania State University

Organizing Committee

Program Co-Chairs

Trent Jaeger, *Pennsylvania State University*
Farinaz Koushanfar, *UCSD*
Ahmad-Reza Sadeghi, *TU Darmstadt*

Program Committee

Najwa Aaraj, *Technology Innovation Institute*
Rob Aitken, *ARM*
Srdjan Capkun, *ETH Zurich*
Massimiliano Corba, *Draper Laboratory*
Jean Paul Degabriele, *TU Darmstadt*
Claudia Diaz, *KU Leuven*
William Enck, *North Carolina State University*
Carl Gunter, *University of Illinois at Urbana-Champaign*
Sharon Hu, *University of Notre Dame*
Florian Kerschbaum, *University of Waterloo*
Kristin Lauter, *Microsoft*
Christoph Lehmann, *UTSouthwestern Medical Center*
Markus Miettinen, *TU Darmstadt*
Azalia Mirhoseini, *Google Brain*
Payman Mohassel, *Facebook*
Pamela Norton, *Borsetta*
Anand Rajan, *Intel*
Farshad Raissi, *Division of Cardiology, UCSD*
Avi Rubin, *Johns Hopkins*
Negin Salajegheh, *Netflix*
Maliheh Shirvanian, *Visa Research*
Jessica Wilkerson, *US Food and Drug Administration*
Fred Wu, *Scripps Health Inpatient Providers*
Dongyan Xu, *Purdue University*
Shouhuai Xu, *University of Texas at San Antonio*
Moti Yung, *Google*

Safer Illinois and RokWall: Privacy Preserving University Health Apps for COVID-19

Vikram Sharma Mailthody*‡, James Wei*‡, Nicholas Chen*‡, Mohammad Behnia*‡, Ruihao Yao*‡, Qihao Wang*‡, Vedant Agrawal*‡, Churan He*‡, Lijian Wang*‡, Leihao Chen*‡, Amit Agarwal*‡, Edward Richter*‡, Wen-Mei Hwu‡, Christopher W. Fletcher‡, Jinjun Xiong†, Andrew Miller‡, Sanjay Patel‡

†C3SR, IBM Research ‡University of Illinois at Urbana-Champaign

*Contributed Equally. Corresponding Email: {vsm2, jinjunx, soc1024, sjp}@illinois.edu

Abstract—**COVID-19 has fundamentally disrupted the way we live. Government bodies, universities, and companies worldwide are rapidly developing technologies to combat the COVID-19 pandemic and safely reopen society. Essential analytics tools such as contact tracing, super-spreader event detection, and exposure mapping require collecting and analyzing sensitive user information. The increasing use of such powerful data-driven applications necessitates a secure, privacy-preserving infrastructure for computation on personal data.**

In this paper, we analyze two such computing infrastructures under development at the University of Illinois at Urbana-Champaign to track and mitigate the spread of COVID-19. First, we present Safer Illinois, a system for decentralized health analytics supporting two applications currently deployed with widespread adoption: digital contact tracing and COVID-19 status cards. Second, we introduce the RokWall architecture for privacy-preserving centralized data analytics on sensitive user data. We discuss the architecture of these systems, design choices, threat models considered, and the challenges we experienced in developing production-ready systems for sensitive data analysis.

I. Introduction

COVID-19 has fundamentally disrupted the way we live. Countless organizations, including government bodies, academic research groups, and companies, are developing and deploying technological solutions to combat the spread of COVID-19 [1], [2], [13], [16], [20], [25], [28]. Worldwide efforts have reinforced that data must play an integral role for safely reopening our communities. Technologies such as digital contact tracing, superspreader event detection and tracking, exposure mapping, migration mapping, live queues at testing locations, risk assessment, and effective stress management [18] have been developed to help better understand and mitigate the spread of disease. These techniques require the collection of sensitive user information, introducing a delicately balanced trade-off between data driven functionality and personal privacy. As more user information is disclosed, the application can provide more accurate, responsive, and personalized experiences; yet the privacy risk increases accordingly [20]. This necessitates trustworthy and secure mechanisms to reduce the risk of compromising sensitive information [15], [17].

We believe that universities can play a crucial role in this area as they are viewed as relatively trustworthy entities [26]. University-led apps can create legitimate trust by establishing public auditors and thorough review processes. Furthermore, universities are not reliant on monetizing private data. We expect this credibility to encourage widespread adoption.

In early summer 2020, University of Illinois at Urbana-Champaign announced plans to resume on-campus instruction for the fall semester. In order to reach this ambitious goal, the university has taken several initiatives, including the development of technologies for managing the spread of COVID-19 using the University of Illinois at Urbana-Champaign RokWire platform [3]. Started in 2018, RokWire's goal is to serve as an open-source platform for smart communities, such as campuses, cities, and organizations. The prime directive of RokWire is to provide valuable functionality to users while enabling fine-grain control of their data. RokWire does not monetize individual user data and is audited by public authorities. With the emergence of COVID-19, we envisioned that RokWire should become a platform for a scalable, privacy-preserving computing infrastructure.

In this paper, we detail two secure, privacy-preserving systems developed in the RokWire platform. First, we describe Safer Illinois, a system for decentralized health analytics and computation, focusing on two of its applications successfully deployed with strong adoption: digital contact tracing based on the recently released Google/Apple protocol and mobile status cards displaying COVID-19 risk. We have overcome significant implementation hurdles to develop a scalable solution, addressing significant gaps in existing protocols. We provide details on technical challenges, remaining shortcomings, and integration into a broader campus workflow.

Safer Illinois's decentralized architecture enables secure and anonymous digital contact tracing, but also limits analytical potential, particularly in aggregated computation. Unfortunately, such population-scale insights are critical to forming responsive strategies for pandemic management and public policy. To address this limitation, we describe RokWall, a generalizable system that can perform centralized privacy-preserving analytics on sensitive user data. RokWall enables advanced analytics such as superspreader event detection, exposure mapping, and risk assessment with strong security and privacy guarantees.

We discuss the overall architecture of RokWall, considering both the Intel SGX platform [9] and AWS Nitro Enclaves [5], and detail several different threat models considered.

We have successfully deployed Safer Illinois within

Workshop on Secure IT Technologies against COVID-19 (CoronaDef) 2021
21 February 2021, Virtual

https://dx.doi.org/10.14722/coronadef.2021.23001
www.ndss-symposium.org

RokWire and released it to university members in advance of the Fall'2020 semester at University of Illinois at Urbana-Champaign. We present some early Safer Illinois app usage statistics in this paper. While the data collected so far is limited, we already observe strong adoption and acceptance of Safer Illinois app among the campus community. Even though Safer@Illinois is an entirely optional service, we measure that approximately 82.5% of the campus population have used the app at least once during Fall'2020. Furthermore, we measure that 53% of these users also voluntarily opt-in to the contact tracing application. Note that this figure likely underestimates the true adoption rate, as the university students currently living away from campus should not be expected to use the app but are counted in the total university population.

The RokWall infrastructure is still undergoing active development and not yet available for public use. During the RokWall architecture implementation process, we encountered and continue to face several technical challenges such as early-stage tool chains, limited availability of trusted execution viroment (TEEs) in the cloud and the lack of COVID-19 specific datasets. To address this, we are actively collaborating with industry and the Initiative for Cryptocurrencies and Contracts (IC3) to develop tools for TEEs. In particular, we have noticed that there is a lot of pending innovation in enclave tool chains and encourage the community to further explore this segment.

To summarize, we make the following main contributions:

1) Safer Illinois, a decentralized computation system, currently supporting a digital contact tracing application for privacy-preserving exposure notification and mobile COVID-19 status cards.
2) RokWall, an architecture for secure, privacy-preserving computing using secure enclaves.
3) Discuss several technical challenges we face in developing secure, privacy-preserving computing systems.

We hope this paper fosters discussion on developing a privacy-preserving computing infrastructure within the research community.

II. Safer Illinois: Decentralized Computation

Exposure notification technologies have become integral components of public health strategies worldwide to curb the spread of COVID-19 infections, often as a digital supplement to manual contract tracing. Early successes at staving off the virus in South Korea and Singapore prompted researchers worldwide to develop protocols for effective contact tracing through smartphone devices without significantly compromising individual privacy. As with other public health strategies to combat the pandemic, such as facemasks and social distancing, exposure notifications rely on high community adoption rates. Simulation-based studies estimate that nearly 60% of individuals within a region need to be actively using digital exposure notification in order to be effective [18]. Our goal with the RokWire project was to develop an exposure notification solution that could be deployed at scale to around 100,000 users within the University mobile app. The University requested a production ready system by August 2020 to inform public health policies throughout the Fall semester.

Safer Illinois is built around a simple concept: it holds a digital version of your COVID-19 health status. If you are tested on campus, or by a provider in the surrounding community, the results are stored on your mobile device. The app then manages the test results by invalidating them after a certain time period determined by county health officials, say 4 days, prompting the user to get re-tested [24]. The results can also be invalidated by a recent encounter with someone whom is later determined to have been infectious at the time, through digital exposure notification. In addition to digital contact tracing, Safer Illinois provides mobile status cards displaying a user's COVID-19 exposure risk. To enter a University space, for example, you might be asked to present your digital health status to show that you pose minimal infection risk to others. Those who opt-out would be asked to show test results by paper or digital image [12][1].

As security-conscious consumers ourselves, we adopted a privacy-centric philosophy from the onset. We chose decentralized, privacy-preserving protocols when available. We keep our codebase open-source, for additional transparency [11]. We adopted a minimal data policy, gathering as little data as possible to meet the functionality of the application.

The Safer Illinois architecture involves five components: (a) exposure notification, (b) integration with testing facilities, (c) administration panel for public health authorities, (d) upload server for positive diagnoses and (e) COVID-19 status cards. The complexity of our system is primarily in the exposure notification system, so we will focus discussion in this paper on that component, with briefer discussions on the others.

The design space for exposure notification includes a choice of proximity estimation (i.e, Bluetooth, WiFi, ultrasonic, GPS, etc), centralized vs. decentralized vs. hybrid architecture, cryptographic protocol, etc. Our approach was to leverage the ongoing work by various security experts and communities worldwide, who were creating open-source protocols for digital exposure notification.

We evaluated three protocols in depth, namely the Temporary Contact Number (or `TCN`) protocol [13], Decentralized Privacy-Preserving Proximity Tracing (or DP-3T) [28] and the Google/Apple Exposure Notification (or GAEN) protocol [1], [2], each of which were summarized briefly below.

TCN protocol generates a Temporary Contact Number (or `TCN`), a psuedo-random identifier derived from a seed, every 15 minutes. Unique `TCNs` are exchanged via Bluetooth Low Energy (or BLE) and stored when two devices come in close proximity. When a user tests positive, a report is sent to a centralized server with the list of `TCNs` exposed. User devices pull this report and determine matching `TCN` to see if the user has been exposed.

DP-3T protocol differs from the TCN protocol on how anonymous IDs are generated (random seed with deterministic hash + truncation vs asymmetric key-pair with deterministic hash ratchet in TCN), what information is reported (`EphID` and seed of all relevant epochs vs public key with start and end time and `tck` for regenerating `TCN` for timeblock) and what information is stored (`hash(EphIDs)` and epoch `i`, proximity, duration and coarse time indication vs `TCN` value).

[1] Please refer [12] for official University policy.

GAEN protocol shares concepts from the DP-3T and TCN protocols, including the use of BLE for proximity detection, with key differences in anonymous ID generation (Rolling Proximity Identifiers (`RPIs`) generated through Temporary Exposure Keys (`TEKs`) every 10 minutes) and reporting of positive test cases (`TEKs` and a timestamp represented as an epoch interval number). Unlike DP-3T and TCN, the GAEN protocol is publicly described, but is still partially closed-source. Access to the implementations are only granted to public health authorities operating at the state or country-level; at the time of this writing, they were not available to our team.

We evaluated these protocols in April and May 2020, a time when these concepts were still undergoing intense development and existing codebases were not yet mature. The open-source code had known shortcomings, such as failing in BLE background mode for iOS devices. We decided to adopt the GAEN approach and build our own implementation, while planning to switch to the Google/Apple implementation in case we received API entitlements from Google and Apple due to our affiliation with a large University[2].

In the overall user workflow of the app, an individual can get tested on campus using one of several testing sites. As a sidenote, we employ a breakthrough saliva-based test developed at University of Illinois at Urbana-Champaign that enables high-throughput testing of up to 10,000 tests per day at low cost [24]. The user presents their University ID when a test is administered, thereby linking their results to a University ID number. Since the user must authenticate within the app using their University credentials, their test results can be linked to the user via the app. The user is notified by the app once the test results are available, typically within an day. Test results can be encrypted using the user's public key and pushed onto the user's device with the user's consent.

If the diagnosis is positive, the user can choose to upload a history of their `TEKs` to a diagnosis upload server. Apps with exposure notification enabled will periodically download published TEKs from the diagnosis upload server, decode the TEKs into rolling proximity identifiers, and check for matches with `RPIs` stored in the local device database. As a further security measure, the upload server will use one-time codes that are electronically shared with the testing sites. A single code is provided alongside each test result to the user device, which is then used to establish a chain-of-authenticity from the testing site to the upload server, via the user device.

If a matching `RPI` is found, an exposure score is calculated using parameters such as duration of exposure, reception and transmission strength of the Bluetooth signal, an estimated onset date of infection, and models of testing efficacy. How such parameters can be used to estimate the risk of infection is an ongoing area of work both within University of Illinois at Urbana-Champaign and elsewhere [25]. RokWire contains an admin control panel that provides public health authorities with limited ability to adjust the parameter weighting system used to score an exposure. If the score is above the threshold, indicating exposure risk, then the user's most recent test result is invalidated, prompting the user to be retested and setting their mobile status card to reflect high risk.

[2]We have not yet received such entitlements

Complementing this workflow is the exposure notification functionality, running continuously on each device. Safer Illinois directly follows the specification defined by the GAEN protocol in generating and exchanging exposure keys. Every day, each user generates a unique Temporary Exposure Key which constructs a user's Rolling Proximity Identifier Key and subsequent `RPIs` to be exchanged with other users. In addition, the `TEK` generates an Associated Encrypted Metadata (`AEM`) Key which, along with an `RPI`, can be used to encrypt a few bytes worth of optional metadata.

Each user broadcasts their `RPI` and corresponding `AEM` with a rolling period of approximately 10 minutes. Whenever a contact is registered within the range of the device's effective Bluetooth range, the device saves the detected `RPI`, contact duration and Bluetooth received signal strength - known as RSSI - to local storage. The device also securely saves the user's daily `TEK` and a timestamp to be uploaded to a server in case the user tests positive for COVID-19.

A. Security

The security and privacy implications of exposure notification protocols have been heavily examined by experts, including the DP3T and TCN communities [13], [28]. We briefly summarize the salient threat models that represent potential vectors for attackers to learn the identity of other users involved in a contact exchange or positive test result. We separate these threats into two categories: 1) *inherent attacks* faced by all Bluetooth proximity tracing systems, and 2) *protocol-dependent attacks* which depend on how the protocol generates and exchanges its anonymous identifiers.

Inherent security considerations: When a user is notified of an exposure event, they may be able to identify the infected individual by correlating their interactions with the reported time of exposure. Even if the application obfuscates the timing with noise, an attacker can create multiple accounts or use multiple phones at different times to cancel or reduce the noise introduced by the system. This threat compounds further if attackers log additional interaction data from infected persons or triangulate data from third-party sources, such as building access logs. Moreover, apps that solely rely on Bluetooth to exchange keys can be susceptible to certain broadcasting threats. If an attacker were to set up powerful transmitters to enhance their effective Bluetooth range, false contacts could be logged. Alternatively, an attacker may set up a Bluetooth jammer that could disrupt communication between devices.

Protocol-dependent security considerations: To begin with, anonymous identifiers must not be linkable to one another nor to the transmitting device. The former is achieved in all protocols discussed through cryptographic pseudorandomness while the latter requires the synchronization of rotations of Bluetooth MAC address and anonymous identifier. Additionally, there remains a threat of replay attacks, where adversaries record anonymous identifiers in one area and replay them in another location causing public disruption or targeting specific individual or area. A solution to this problem is to allow the attacker to duplicate and transmit identifiers, but inhibit notification to users who receive these fraudulent signals [21]. All three protocols mitigate this issue to some extent by incorporating timestamps while checking for exposed matches.

B. Implementation Challenges

We designed our approach to exposure notification with an emphasis on wide-scale deployment. Ideally, the protocol could be adopted with minimal impact to users by providing ease of use, minimal energy consumption and privacy and security guarantees. We picked the Google/Apple API for a variety of reasons. The API was more stable at the time we were examining the various alternatives, and early experience with the protocol would pave the path if we were later granted entitlements to use the API within our application. When we embarked on the project, we did not have entitlements to the GAEN API, so we set out to develop our own implementation of the protocol while addressing the known issues suffered by DP3-T and others. Below, we describe some of the challenges encountered in implementing a scalable, production-ready system at the application level.

iOS Background Advertising: Moving an iOS application to background mode restricts its Bluetooth advertisement packets. Namely, instead of advertising a standard service UUID, transmissions are moved to an "overflow area" where they are only observable by a device explicitly scanning for it. Since all iOS background apps on the same device share the same overflow area, there is no guarantee that the app is advertising a preset bitmask. Moreover, there is a possibility of collision if two Bluetooth services from different apps set the same bitmask, thus an app may detect a different service than intended. Currently, we do not have a solution to this problem; however, the likelihood of such conflict is very low, as few other apps (if any) advertise Bluetooth in the background.

iOS-iOS Background Communication: In Android, a callback can be set up to detect the overflow bitmask of an iOS background device. On iOS devices, however, this callback would only be triggered if the screen is turned on and beacon ranging is enabled. We found this can be circumvented by sending a local notification, which will illuminate the screen for 10 seconds at the expense of battery life.

Bluetooth Mac Address Changes: It is essential to align Bluetooth MAC rotations with each `RPI` change. Otherwise, an attacker can correlate `RPIs` coming from a single user. Unfortunately, as of Android 6.0 and iOS 8, an application cannot control the timing of its Bluetooth MAC address changes or even identify when this change occurs. However, we found that the Bluetooth MAC address changes every time the advertising service restarts on Android. We took advantage of this finding in our Android implementation by restarting the advertising service to obtain a new MAC address every time a new `RPI` is generated. Unfortunately, we did not observe a similar phenomena for iOS, and it remains an unsolved issue.

iOS Background Execution: With iOS devices, we found it difficult to keep an app from being suspended by the OS when in background mode. Suspended apps will not be able to record or transmit `RPIs`.

Battery Efficiency: Constant Bluetooth scanning and advertising takes a substantial toll on battery life. While the GAEN protocol sets scanning intervals at 5 minutes apart, Android and iOS SDKs provide little control over these intervals. Android provides 3 scan settings, but the actual times may differ by manufacturer, while no such options are documented for iOS. Even in the most conservative power-saving state, scanning occurs every couple seconds. Table I shows the average battery drain in % per hour across iOS and Android. We set Safer Illinois to be the only application running with it constantly scanning another device. However, these numbers may vary by other factors including device usage, other devices scanned, OS level, and device model. From Table I, the Safer Illinois app consumes reasonable amount of energy over time depending on the OS and device.

TABLE I. AVERAGE BATTERY DRAIN PER HOUR OF SAFER ILLINOIS

Device	Safer Illinois On	Safer Illinois Off
Google Pixel 3	1.12%	0.47%
iPhone X	4.8%	0.59%

III. ROKWALL: CENTRALIZED ENCLAVE COMPUTATION

The Safer Illinois application demonstrates privacy-preserving computation on sensitive user data within a decentralized framework. However, desirable services such as exposure mapping, secure data transfer, and safety status verification require centralized analysis. In comparison with decentralized implementations, a centralized infrastructure requires users to place greater trust in service providers' benevolence and honesty. While reasonable for a highly transparent university organization, users may justifiably remain skeptical of private businesses or other third parties accessing their data within the RokWire system. Thus, we required a secure, privacy-preserving computing infrastructure inside RokWire for centralized analytics.

To satisfy this need, RokWall is guided by the following fundamental principles: *(a) Privacy:* Sensitive user data is only used by services authorized by the user. Users have assurance that a third-party service provider cannot exploit beyond the declared capabilities. *(b) Security:* No party, including service providers and manufacturers, can access data beyond the computation's output, and *(c) Accountability:* Users or public auditors can review the code bases, verify program binaries and ensure it meets all security and privacy guidelines.

Exposure Mapping Application: We present a COVID-19 exposure mapping application in Figure 1 as an example of privacy-preserving computation on sensitive data. Exposure mapping aggregates user location data to calculate a heat map, visualizing the risk of infection exposure. This application helps health authorities assess the likelihood of superspreader events and warn the general public of high risk areas. GPS location data is highly sensitive, so the service provider should follow previously discussed fundamental principles: *(a)* Perform only a minimal set of queries on the user's location data to preserve privacy, *(b)* Ensure the data is secure and used only for exposure mapping application purposes, and *(c)* Enable auditors to verify these guidelines with public information such as output report to hold the service provider accountable.

To this end, we present RokWall, a secure architecture (see § III-A) for sensitive data computation. We apply RokWall to COVID-19 exposure mapping while preserving the desired security and privacy guarantees for user location information. We analyze various threat models (see § III-B) considered for the exposure mapping application and RokWall's protection against various attack vectors. Finally, we present various

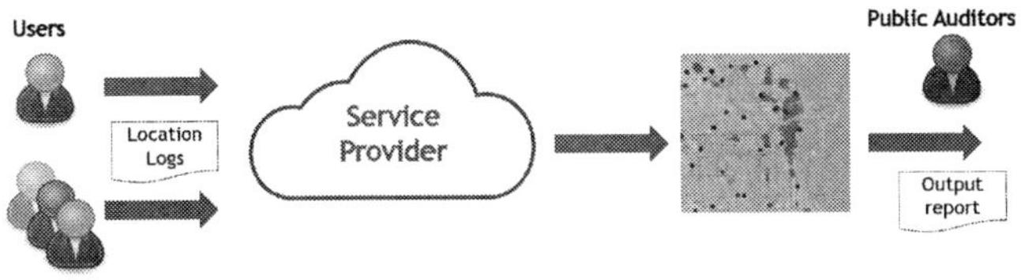

Fig. 1. Exposure mapping application on sensitive location data. User uploads sensitive location logs to the service provider. The service provider generates an exposure map along with an output report for public auditors to audit.

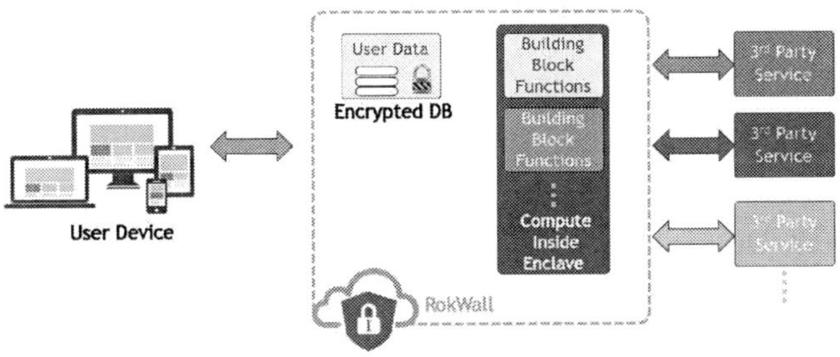

Fig. 2. Overall strawman architecture of RokWall is shown.

technological challenges (see § III-C) faced during deployment and provide potential solutions.

A. *RokWall Architecture*

Guided by the preceding principles of security, privacy, and accountability, we primarily considered two established solutions for secure computation: multi-party computation (MPC) and enclave based trusted execution environments (hardware [9]/software [5] enclaves) While both options could potentially satisfy our required standards, we noted that enclave tool chains were considerably more mature and production-ready [19], [29]. Due to the time sensitive nature of our mission and performance requirement, we decided to proceed with an enclave-based architecture. In the future, we may reevaluate the merits of MPC and consider supporting it as an alternative.

Figure 2 provides a high level illustration of the RokWall architecture using secure enclaves. The RokWall architecture supports sensitive data computation by leveraging secure enclaves. We considered two trusted execution environments (TEEs) - Intel's SGX, a hardware enclave, and the more recent AWS Nitro software enclave [5]. In theory, the choice of platform may be application specific, as each platform imposes different security/performance tradeoffs. RokWall will eventually support both of these platforms, enabling use case specific choice. However, we will limit the threat model discussion to the Intel-SGX platform as it is currently more established and thoroughly vetted.

All data analysis, such as exposure mapping or COVID-19 risk calculation, occurs entirely within the confines of the secure enclaves. Each individual data analytics function is referred to as a "building block function" and are statically linked with enclaves. Each building block function publicly declares a hash of its program binary and each secure enclave generates an output public key. Source code of all the building block functions and APIs are planned to be open sourced and thoroughly audited.

RokWall allows third-party services to upload information, such as a health authority's API updating test results of a specific user using a secure channel. Users upload sensitive data to the RokWall server using a secure encrypted channel such as Transport Layer Security (TLS) along with the enclave public key and hash of program binary for the user authorized application. Inside RokWall, user data is stored in an encrypted database. During the query execution, only the building block function or third-party services whose hash of the program binary matches with the user-approved application can temporarily decrypt and access data within the secure enclave. Critically, this guarantees that unencrypted data never leaves an enclave. An unauthorized building block execution will result in the generation of a useless result.

Remote attestation in RokWall: Remote Attestation allows cryptographic verification of the code allegedly executed inside an TEE. RokWall uses a 3-party EPID based remote attestation mechanism for Intel-SGX hardware [9] and the AWS KMS service for Nitro enclaves [5]. We reduce verification effort needed for end-user devices by publicly providing verified attestation report generated by the RokWall enclave. This report would contain information about the enclave code (given by MRENCLAVE in case of SGX) as well as the public-private key pair generated during enclave initialization. Auditors (or even users) can verify that the MRENCLAVE information in the report matches the publicly available MRENCLAVE generated by building/compiling the enclave code, vetted by interested parties. The procedure is similar when RokWall uses Nitro enclaves instead of SGX.

Exposure Mapping Function in RokWall: RokWall uses the Intel SGX platform to provide a trusted execution environment for the exposure mapping application. Users upload sensitive location logs using TLS to the RokWall encrypted database along with a hash of the exposure mapping binary and the enclave's public key. On a regular interval (in this example, once per day), the exposure mapping enclave generates and publishes a heat map as output on a public server along with a signature and report for remote attestation. The user app can pull this output from the public server, then verify the signature.

B. *End-to-end Chain Of Trust In RokWall*

Security and privacy guarantees are primary principles of the RokWall design. We consider a three-tiered threat model: (1) *network attackers*, (2) *client attackers* and (3) *service provider attackers.* To safeguard against network attackers, clients communicate with the RokWall server via TLS channel.

Unfortunately, we cannot currently prevent client attackers from running malicious code or flooding the system with spoofed data. This is a known problem on systems that do not require user verification. One possible solution, employed by electronic voting systems [22], allows an authority to register public keys of users. University officials could distribute public keys to community members interested in using the service.

Service provider attackers can be classified into three sub-categories: *(1) server-software*, where a service provider runs malicious user-level software, *(2) server-kernel*, where a service provider runs malicious kernel-level software, and *(3) server-hardware*, where a service provider has physical access to the server hardware.

Server-software attacks: Server-software level attacks assume that the service provider is limited to user-level privileges. This includes writing and running malicious code, but excludes kernel privileges or hardware attacks. Server-software attacks can generally be prevented by using SGX enclaves. Remote attestation enforces transparency and enables public auditors to review code, while data sealing ensures that the service provider cannot access raw, decrypted user data. One remaining attack is an isolation attack, where a service provider runs the query with only a single victim user's location logs. This query yields a heatmap exposing the victim's location history, even though the code would pass an audit.

RokWall addresses this with a two step solution: *(1)* employ non-volatile counters such that a location log can only be used for a heatmap one time, and *(2)* output a hash of location logs included so a user can verify that their data was used for generating a given heatmap. Then, if a service provider commits an isolation attack, the victim's data will necessarily not be present in the official heatmap. If a user finds that their data is not present in an officially published heatmap, they can then report the service provider to RokWall administrators.

Server-kernel attacks: Server-kernel attacks expand upon user-level code execution and permit the attacker to inspect memory management within SGX. This level of attack can theoretically allow privileged side channel attacks, exposing memory access patterns even in sealed data [30]. We avoid leaking information to these attackers by ensuring data oblivious execution and guaranteeing a constant runtime regardless of input size. In the case of exposure mapping, this entails unsealing and resealing the entire heatmap every time data is updated. RokWall currently does not defend against microarchitectural attacks (like cache-timing attacks) as they pose far more sophisticated adversaries.

Server-hardware attacks: Server-hardware attacks involve physically probing or tampering with the enclave's system hardware. We generally expect the cloud service provider to ensure the physical security of their servers. We are still investigating additional counter measures to address these attacks and will address them in the future.

C. Technical challenges

Computation on sensitive data raises a number of practical constraints that manifest when implementing a production-ready system. We describe some of the challenges we encountered while developing RokWall system and propose solutions.

Monotonic counter on Intel Servers: Rollback attacks present a general security problem for enclave solutions. An adversary OS can restart the service with an outdated version of sealed data and leverage it to leak user information. Intel provides a native SGX monotonic counter service to tackle this problem, while AWS Nitro enclaves do not support non-volatile counters. However, SGX cloud services such as IBM Cloud and Microsoft Azure are currently built on Intel Xeon E3 server-grade processors, which do not support the Intel Management Engine required for enabling SGX monotonic counter service. Alternatives to SGX's native monotonic counter have been proposed, including distributed rollback protection systems such as ROTE [23]. Other solutions include the migration of the counter service to a third-party trusted source or a BFT distributed network such as CCF [27]. RokWall uses the CCF network to provide non-volatile monotonic counter support for its enclaves.

SGX Memory management: Intel SGX provides data sealing for encrypting and saving confidential enclave information to persistent storage. Sealing comes in two forms, Enclave Identity based vs. Signing Identity based. Data sealed with Enclave Identity (MRENCLAVE) will only allow other instances of the same enclave to unseal, whereas Signing Identity allow other versions and builds of the enclave to unseal. RokWall currently uses Enclave Identity for sealing to prevent successive data encroachment; user authorization should apply to an application as it is currently described. Signing Identity would allow future versions of the enclave signed by the same Signing Identity to access sealed data. However, Intel SGX sealing is not intended for large data objects. In addition to performance degradation, crossing EPC memory bounds requires memory management from the enclave itself.

Challenges with Remote Attestation: A major challenge in implementing remote attestation is ensuring reproducible builds between auditors, clients and the RokWall server, as inconsistent builds can raise false MRENCLAVE mismatches. Furthermore, the auditors (or users) must use identical backend libraries/packages as described in the attestation report in their build process. In practice, this may pose a significantly inconvenient task for auditors. Additionally, available tool chains such as containers for remote attestation and reproducible builds are far from production quality, especially for use with the Intel SGX platform. To address this unmet need, we are working closely with the Initiative for Cryptocurrencies and Contracts (IC3) to enable reproducible enclave builds for the purpose of TEEs [10].

Testing Dataset: When developing the exposure mapping building block, we struggled to find an appropriate, publicly available GPS dataset for simulating infection dynamics. We ultimately decided to test RokWall's location related queries on the T-Drive GPS trajectories data [31]. T-Drive records coordinates for 10,000 taxi cabs in Beijing over the course of a week. Some comparative advantages of the T-Drive dataset are its high number of entities, dense population concentration, and high frequency of reporting.

While the T-Drive dataset is sufficient for initial testing, it has several key limitations. Critically, the data isn't perfectly representative of our eventual use cases since the entities are vehicles, rather than people. Taxis are confined to roads and don't enter buildings so we cannot run indoor, intra-building analysis. Moreover, this data can't facilitate algorithmic parameter tuning, such as heatmap granularity or super-spreader event thresholds, because of differences in population density and entity size. Thus, we will likely need to collect organic human data for fine tuning.

D. Additional RokWall Services

In addition to enabling the exposure mapping use case, we are particularly excited by the RokWall infrastructure's potential for wider generalization. We are currently investigating two additional timely use cases which will depend on RokWall for secure, privacy-preserving computation.

Secure Data Transfer: During the Safer Illinois deployment process, we encountered a pressing need for a secure data transfer mechanism. We found that, in practice, users often changed their mobile devices due to upgrades and repairs. In these situations, a user would need to recover credentials and transfer sensitive personal data, like stored contact tracing RPIs and past test results, between devices. To facilitate this process, we currently provide a mechanism to transfer data between two devices using QR codes and Bluetooth. However, this design has limitations as it requires both devices to be accessible and functional, which may not necessarily be the case. To address this problem, enclave data sealing and remote attestation can enable certifiably secure data storage and retrieval. This use case will require additional investigation, but we hope to enable it in the near future.

Virtual Status Card: As previously described, the Safer Illinois app is intended to complement frequent testing in minimizing the spread of COVID-19. However, it is important to acknowledge that a university community is exceptionally conducive for these technologies due to high tech literacy and device ownership of its inhabitants; unfortunately, expanding operation to the outside world entails a very different set of practical assumptions. Notably, consider scenarios in which residents may not have access to a personal mobile device. For example, young children or low income households may not own a mobile phone. Subject to these limitations, we are exploring methods to build a virtual status card application to determine COVID safety status using untrusted client devices.

We believe that RokWall can enable this service in a secure manner. As in the exposure mapping use case, data sealing ensures that plaintext medical records can never be accessed outside of the secure enclave, even by a compromised service provider. Furthermore, remote attestation can facilitate credible rate limits or user alert policies.

IV. Discussion

A. *Safer Illinois Usage Statistics*

Following a four month development process, Safer Illinois was deployed at the start of the Fall 2020 semester. Here, we present real-world data collected from live community usage.

The University of Illinois at Urbana-Champaign has a campus population of approximately 60,000 [14]. Though Safer Illinois is an entirely optional service, we measure that approximately 82.5% of the campus population have used the app at least once during Fall'2020. Furthermore, we expect that this number may still be an underestimate of relevant app adoption. After all, university students currently living away from campus, perhaps due to safety concerns and the current prevalence of online coursework, should not be expected to use the app but are counted in the total university population.

Over the time period of 11/30/2020 to 12/15/20, we recorded that 53% of these Safer Illinois users had voluntarily enabled exposure notification. Additionally, this figure is a strict underestimate of the true value because usage data is sampled only when a user undergoes their routine COVID-19 test. Since Safer Illinois consumes a substantial amount of battery, not all users enable exposure notification functionality all the time. Therefore, users who temporarily disabled exposure notification at time of test are falsely counted as permanently disabling the service. Please note that the Safer Illinois app and exposure notification enrollment are optional, opt-in services and not required to access any university services. We are particularly heartened to see such a large portion of the population opt-in voluntarily, demonstrating significant trust and appreciation for efforts responding to COVID-19.

During the same time period, we observed 19,439 average unique users using the Safer Illinois app per 4-day interval, either to check the test results or access building services using their status card. Because the university requires each member to test once every 4 days (4 days without a test automatically results in status change [12]), we present our data as averaged over 4-day intervals to approximate a cross section of the population. Although the average unique users may initially seem to be a small fraction of the campus population, note that for this period, all classes were held entirely online and many students had left campus.

In summary, this data demonstrates substantial public interest and acceptance for the digital contact tracing and building access status card services. However, we still have to collect more data to determine the efficacy of digital contact tracing and we hope to address this question in the near future.

B. *Availability of secure enclaves in the cloud*

Confidential computing infrastructure has been evolving for more than two decades. For much of that time, though, its general availability and support system with cloud vendors, such as Amazon AWS, Microsoft Azure, Google Cloud and IBM Cloud, was limited. However, perhaps instigated by the pandemic, we have recently observed burgeoning deployment of secure, privacy-preserving cloud computing services. Although current tool chains and software are immature, this trend demonstrates marked demand for such solutions.

At the time of writing, IBM Cloud and Microsoft Azure support Intel-SGX [9] based hardware TEEs while Google uses the AMD SEV [4] hardware TEE for confidential computing projects [6]–[8]. Meanwhile, AWS software-based Nitro enclaves are both serverless and scalable [5]. Nitro enclaves provide hardened and constrained virtual machines (VMs). The restricted enclave VM solely interacts with its host instance via a secure local channel. Like many hardware enclaves, Nitro provides a cryptographic remote attestation service.

While the hardware TEEs, such as Intel SGX or AMD SEV, charge an additional price ranging between $4-$30 per instance per month, software enclaves typically come at no cost to the developer. Additionally, in contrast with hardware enclaves, Nitro offers flexible computing resource allocation, including memory and CPU cores. The downside of software enclaves, however, is that they assume a weaker threat model. When using a software enclave, one needs to implicitly trust the service provider for all of remote attestation, data sealing, key management and software infrastructure.

C. *Why design both decentralized and centralized systems?*

Contact tracing can be implemented in a decentralized or centralized fashion, which has traditionally forced developers into making a trade-off between user privacy and analytic capability. While previous works frequently favor decentralized implementations due to privacy concerns, RokWall can enable centralized data analysis while upholding user privacy.

In order to develop a functional and reliable contact tracing system by start of the Fall 2020 semester, Safer Illinois leveraged preexisting GAEN APIs in a decentralized system. However, a decentralized architecture carries inherent limitations that can be solved by centralized analysis on user data. For digital contact tracing, centralized GPS data analysis can help identify infection hotspots, remedy bluetooth connectivity issues, and enable cross-time analysis. Moreover, centralized systems can absolve reliance on user-owned client devices, as described in Virtual Status Card. We envision eventually migrating parts of Safer Illinois to RokWall, enabling richer analysis and broader functionality.

V. Conclusion

In this work, we introduced Safer Illinois and the RokWall architecture under development in the University of Illinois at Urbana-Champaign's RokWire platform. Safer Illinois enables privacy-preserving digital contact tracing and COVID-19 status cards with decentralized computation. Meanwhile, RokWall presents a general framework upon enclave TEEs for secure, privacy-preserving centralized analytics. We detailed our design choices and threat models considered while implementing a production-ready system. We also presented several technological challenges and lessons learned from deploying these systems in practice. We hope this work fosters discussion in developing a privacy-preserving computing infrastructure.

Acknowledgement

We would like to thank all of the volunteers and staff of University of Illinois at Urbana-Champaign who helped in many ways during this pandemic. We particularly appreciate the help of the Engineering IT team, the Inabyte team, Professor John Paul, Professor William Sullivan, Todd Nelson, Nickolas Vance, Isaac Galvan, Edward Delaporte, Tracy Smith, Mary Stevens, Melvin Fenner, Kathryn Courtney, Nerla Jean-Louis and Sylvain Bellemare of IC3. This work is partially supported by IBM-ILLINOIS Center for Cognitive Computing Systems Research (C3SR) and University of Illinois. We would also like to thank the workshop organizers, PC chairs and reviewers for making this workshop happen.

References

[1] "Apple: Privacy-Preserving Contact Tracing."

[2] "Google Exposure Notifications: Using technology to help public health authorities fight COVID-19."

[3] "Illinois Rokwire, https://rokwire.org/," 2018.

[4] "AMD Secure Encrypted Virtualization (SEV)," 2020.

[5] "AWS Nitro Enclave, https://aws.amazon.com/ec2/nitro/nitro-enclaves/," 2020.

[6] "Azure Confidential Computing. https://azure.microsoft.com/en-us/solutions/confidential-compute/," 2020.

[7] "Google Confidential Computing. https://cloud.google.com/confidential-computing," 2020.

[8] "IBM Cloud Confidential Computing. https://www.ibm.com/cloud/learn/confidential-computing," 2020.

[9] "Intel® Software Guard Extensions. ," 2020.

[10] "Reproducible build for enclaves in trusted execution environment https://github.com/initc3/teeons," 2020.

[11] "Safer Illinois App Open Source Code, https://github.com/rokwire/safer-illinois-app," 2020.

[12] "Safer Illinois App, https://covid19.illinois.edu/health-and-support/safer-illinois-app/," 2020.

[13] "TCN Protocol. https://github.com/TCNCoalition/TCN," March 2020.

[14] "University of Illinois Urbana-Champaign Campus Facts https://illinois.edu/about/facts.html," 2020.

[15] S. Altmann, L. Milsom, H. Zillessen, R. Blasone, FredericGerdon, R. Bach, F. Kreuter, D. Nosenzo, S. Toussaert, and J. Abelery, "Acceptability of app-based contact tracing for COVID-19:Cross-country survey evidence," May 2020.

[16] J. Bay, J. Kek, A. Tan, C. S. Hau, L. Yongquan, J. Tan, and T. A. Quy, "BlueTrace: A privacy-preserving protocol for community-driven contact tracing across borders," April 2020.

[17] H. Cho, D. Ippolito, and Y. W. Yu, "Contact Tracing Mobile Apps for COVID-19: Privacy Considerations and Related Trade-offs," 2020.

[18] L. Ferretti, C. Wymant, M. Kendall, L. Zhao, A. Nurtay, L. Abeler-Dörner, M. Parker, D. Bonsall, and C. Fraser, "Quantifying SARS-CoV-2 transmission suggests epidemic control with digital contact tracing."

[19] N. Hynes, R. Cheng, and D. Song, "Efficient Deep Learning on Multi-Source Private Data," ArXiv, vol. abs/1807.06689, 2018.

[20] T. Li, Jackie, Yang, C. Faklaris, J. King, Y. Agarwal, L. Dabbish, and J. I. Hong, "Decentralized is not risk-free: Understanding public perceptions of privacy-utility trade-offs in COVID-19 contact-tracing apps," 2020.

[21] P. Madhusudan, P. Miao, L. Ren, , and V. Venkatakrishnan, "ConTrail: Privacy-Preserving Secure Contact Tracing ," June 2020.

[22] Madise, Ülle AND Martens, Tarvi, "E-voting in Estonia 2005. The first practice of country-wide binding Internet voting in the world," in Electronic Voting 2006 – 2nd International Workshop, Co-organized by Council of Europe, ESF TED, IFIP WG 8.6 and E-Voting.CC. Gesellschaft für Informatik e.V., 2006.

[23] S. Matetic, M. Ahmed, K. Kostiainen, A. Dhar, D. Sommer, A. Gervais, A. Juels, and S. Capkun, "ROTE: Rollback Protection for Trusted Execution," in 26th USENIX Security Symposium (USENIX Security 17). USENIX Association, Aug. 2017.

[24] D. Ranoa, R. Holland, F. Alnaji, K. Green, L. Wang, C. Brooke, M. Burke, T. Fan, and P. Hergenrother, "Saliva-Based Molecular Testing for SARS-CoV-2 that Bypasses RNA Extraction," Cold Spring Harbor Laboratory Press, United States, WorkingPaper, Jun. 2020.

[25] R. Raskar, G. Nadeau, J. Werner, R. Barbar, A. Mehra, G. Harp, M. Leopoldseder, B. Wilson, D. Flakoll, P. Vepakomma, D. Pahwa, R. Beaudry, E. Flores, M. Popielarz, A. Bhatia, A. Nuzzo, M. Gee, J. Summet, R. Surati, B. Khastgir, F. M. Benedetti, K. Vilcans, S. Leis, and K. Louisy, "COVID-19 Contact-Tracing Mobile Apps: Evaluation and Assessment for Decision Makers," 2020.

[26] B. Roberts and et al., "COVID-19 and Technology Perceptions by Key Demographics," June 2020.

[27] M. Russinovich, E. Ashton, C. Avanessians, M. Castro, A. Chamayou, S. Clebsch, M. Costa, C. Fournet, M. Kerner, S. Krishna, J. Maffre, T. Moscibroda, K. Nayak, O. Ohrimenko, F. Schuster, R. Schwartz, A. Shamis, O. Vrousgou, and C. M. Wintersteiger, "CCF: A Framework for Building Confidential Verifiable Replicated Services," Microsoft, Tech. Rep. MSR-TR-2019-16, April 2019.

[28] C. Troncoso, M. Payer, J.-P. Hubaux, M. Salath, J. Larus, E. Bugnion, W. Lueks, T. Stadler, A. Pyrgelis, D. Antonioli, L. Barman, S. Chatel, K. Paterson, S. Capkun, D. Basin, D. Jackson, B. Preneel, N. Smart, D. Singelee, A. Abidin, S. Guerses, M. Veale, C. Cremers, R. Binns, and T. Wiegand, "Decentralized privacy-preserving proximity tracing. https://github.com/DP-3T/documents," April 2020.

[29] N. Volgushev, M. Schwarzkopf, B. Getchell, M. Varia, A. Lapets, and A. Bestavros, "Conclave: Secure Multi-Party Computation on Big Data," in Proceedings of the Fourteenth EuroSys Conference 2019, ser. EuroSys '19, New York, NY, USA, 2019.

[30] Y. Xu, W. Cui, and M. Peinado, "Controlled-Channel Attacks: Deterministic Side Channels for Untrusted Operating Systems," in 2015 IEEE Symposium on Security and Privacy, 2015.

[31] J. Yuan, Y. Zheng, X. Xie, and G. Sun, "Driving with knowledge from the physical world," 2011.

Rapid Cybersecurity Assessment System for Small Business' COVID Move to Online

Tracy Tam
RMIT University
tracy.tam@student.rmit.edu.au

Asha Rao
RMIT University
asha.rao@rmit.edu.au

Joanne Hall
RMIT University
joanne.hall@rmit.edu.au

***Abstract*—COVID19 has made small businesses around the world rapidly adopt new online sales channels and tools. In this digital push for survival, the cybersecurity of the new systems has likely been forgotten. An existing global cybersecurity skills shortage means traditional individualised security assessments for these newly digital businesses are not practical. This paper proposes a web based self-assessment system (SE-CAP) to enable small business owners to conduct their own cybersecurity assessments. Designed with rapid deployability in mind, SE-CAP uses proven web based technologies to deliver a new solution to help small businesses become cyber-safe. The design of SE-CAP takes into account small business issues around record keeping, time constraints and poor technical literacy. The generic nature of the system allows SE-CAP's host organisation to customise and extend the self-assessment system beyond its initial scope. Challenges with industry cybersecurity knowledge gaps prevent SE-CAP's completeness. However, these gaps could be filled, in the interim, by the host organisation.**

I. Introduction

COVID19 has dramatically impacted the social fabric of society. It took away the traditional foot traffic, relied on by small businesses (0-19 employees [5]), by requiring social distancing and lockdown of our communities. Small businesses have had to, with little prior experience, quickly move online, or expand their online business to survive [26], [21]. As per the Australian Bureau of Statistics, in 2018, less than 40% of Australian small businesses derived more than half of their income from online sales [7].

Cybersecurity may have been missed in this rush to an online presence. Each new online storefront introduces a new suite of attack possibilities, as is evident from news reports of criminals taking advantage of opportunities and targeting new vulnerabilities as they emerge [12].

Compounding this challenge is the global cybersecurity skills shortage [4], [1]. There are currently insufficient cybersecurity professionals to conduct traditional one-on-one security audits for these newly digitised small businesses. An alternative approach is needed to protect small businesses.

Small business accounts for a significant portion of private-sector employment (in Australia, >40% [16]) and new job creation [30]. With employment fast becoming a key aspect of post-COVID recovery, the protection of small businesses is paramount. This will, in addition, protect the privacy and identity of the small business' customers, preventing serious personal, financial and emotional impacts [3].

Finally, very few small businesses have qualified IT support in-house [7]. (This trend is echoed with only a small portion of small businesses conducting security tasks in-house [18], or have an in-house qualified IT security expert [17].) With only a small proportion of small business engaged in a technical business venture [35], [6], the majority will need extra assistance with cybersecurity.

To address this urgent need to secure small businesses, we propose a Small Enterprise Cybersecurity Assessment Platform (SE-CAP). SE-CAP is a technology agnostic, rapidly deployable, online self-assessment system that will help small business owners protect themselves. SE-CAP's assessment process targets small business owners without a cybersecurity resource or the technical knowledge in-house to conduct a cybersecurity assessment, providing cybersecurity triage until the cybersecurity industry and official bodies fill the gap long term.

II. A Solution for An Unprecedented Time

SE-CAP is a self-assessment website intended to help small business owners create an IT asset inventory and to encourage incremental actions to mitigate basic cybersecurity vulnerabilities. The usage context and assessment logics to achieve this aim are illustrated in Figure 1 and Figure 2 respectively.

A. System Use

Primary user interactions with, and data inputs to, the self-assessment system are shown in Figure 1. The owners, through a browser, visit the SE-CAP URL. The small business owner inputs the existing IT device status of the business into the guided webpages. SE-CAP then matches that device and its configuration, with the applicable security controls. The small business is then linked to step by step instructions on how to implement the relevant security controls.

When the business owner implements the suggested controls, the control completion status is noted. At the end of the session, SE-CAP outputs a cybersecurity control status and inventory report for the small business owner to keep. Whenever their IT landscape changes, the business owner can

Workshop on Secure IT Technologies against COVID-19 (CoronaDef) 2021
21 February 2021, Virtual

https://dx.doi.org/10.14722/coronadef.2021.23004
www.ndss-symposium.org

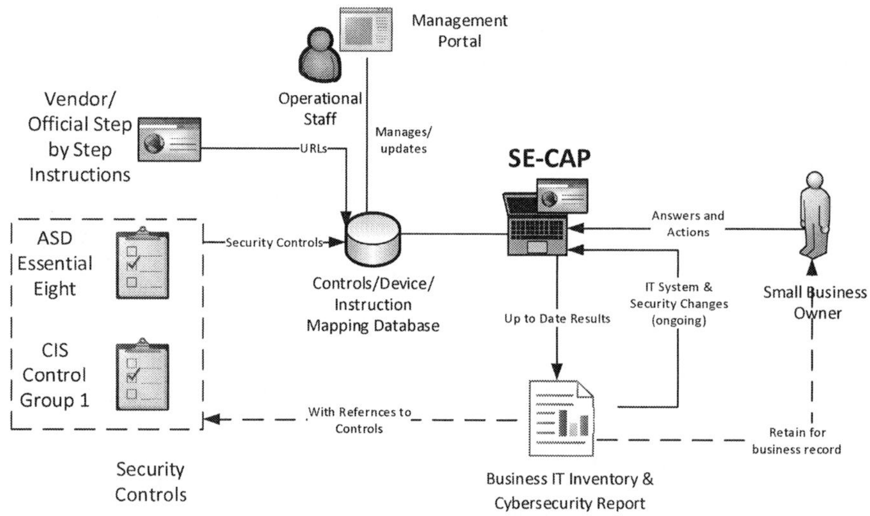

Fig. 1. SE-CAP User and Data Interactions Model. Business owners interact with the SE-CAP via the publicly available website, ingesting and exporting human readable text files. This interaction is repeated if the user needs to update a new inventory detail. At the backend, SE-CAP is supported by a database which contains the mapping between security controls, devices and instructions to secure devices. User and data interaction steps are described in section II-A.

re-visit SE-CAP, load the old report into the webpage and generate a new report by changing their answers.

Supporting the SE-CAP webpage content is an internal database. This database is populated with current mappings between device relationship and cybersecurity controls, and between cybersecurity controls and official instructions on how to execute the controls. An operator is also responsible for maintenance of the mappings via a management portal, allowing for out-of-date mappings to be updated.

B. Small Business Design Factors

The design of SE-CAP is based on the key small business factors given below:

- Webpage as delivery mechanism: The choice of a well-known technology pattern, a website, makes SE-CAP:
  - deployable by any host organisation with an interest in small business cybersecurity, including non-technical official bodies.
  - reachable by any small business owner who has access to a web browser.
- Target Audience: Non-technical small business owners. The majority of small business owners have no technical background or are unfamiliar with technology [7], [31].
- Target Devices: Common consumer-grade devices, rather than enterprise grade products. Many micro and small businesses use consumer-grade IT products and/or share private devices with their business [9], [2].
- Reuse Before New Advice: The default approach is to re-use any official industry step by step instructions if available. This strategy avoids out of date advice and the overhead of a host organisation maintaining a separate set of instructions.

C. How Will the Self-Assessment Work?

Central to SE-CAP is a set of questions that guides small business owners through the process of securing each asset. The logic of the assessment that the user sees is illustrated in Figure 2, and described below.

1) Vetting Users: Before starting, the SE-CAP website asks the small business owner (the user) simple questions around the business size and IT complexity. If the user is shown to require more sophisticated assistance beyond consumer-grade computer devices, i.e. beyond SE-CAP scope, they are advised to contact cybersecurity professionals.

Once the business is found to be in scope, SE-CAP prompts the user to take stock of the number and types of business devices, network connections and processes. The SE-CAP then delves deeper by asking questions around hardware, operating system and applications. Based on the device characteristics, the internal database will dynamically generate a list of cybersecurity actions that are relevant. The cybersecurity control recommendations are based on existing cybersecurity industry standards; further discussion is in Section II-E.

2) Individual Devices - One at a Time: Each list of cybersecurity control actions is tied to a specific business device/process. For example, a device should have updates applied regularly. If the user states a computer is running on Windows, they are reminded to turn on automatic updates OR schedule a regular task each week to perform the update for that device. Instructions on how to perform the actions are linked to external official instruction sites. In this example, the instruction will link to Microsoft's official help site on

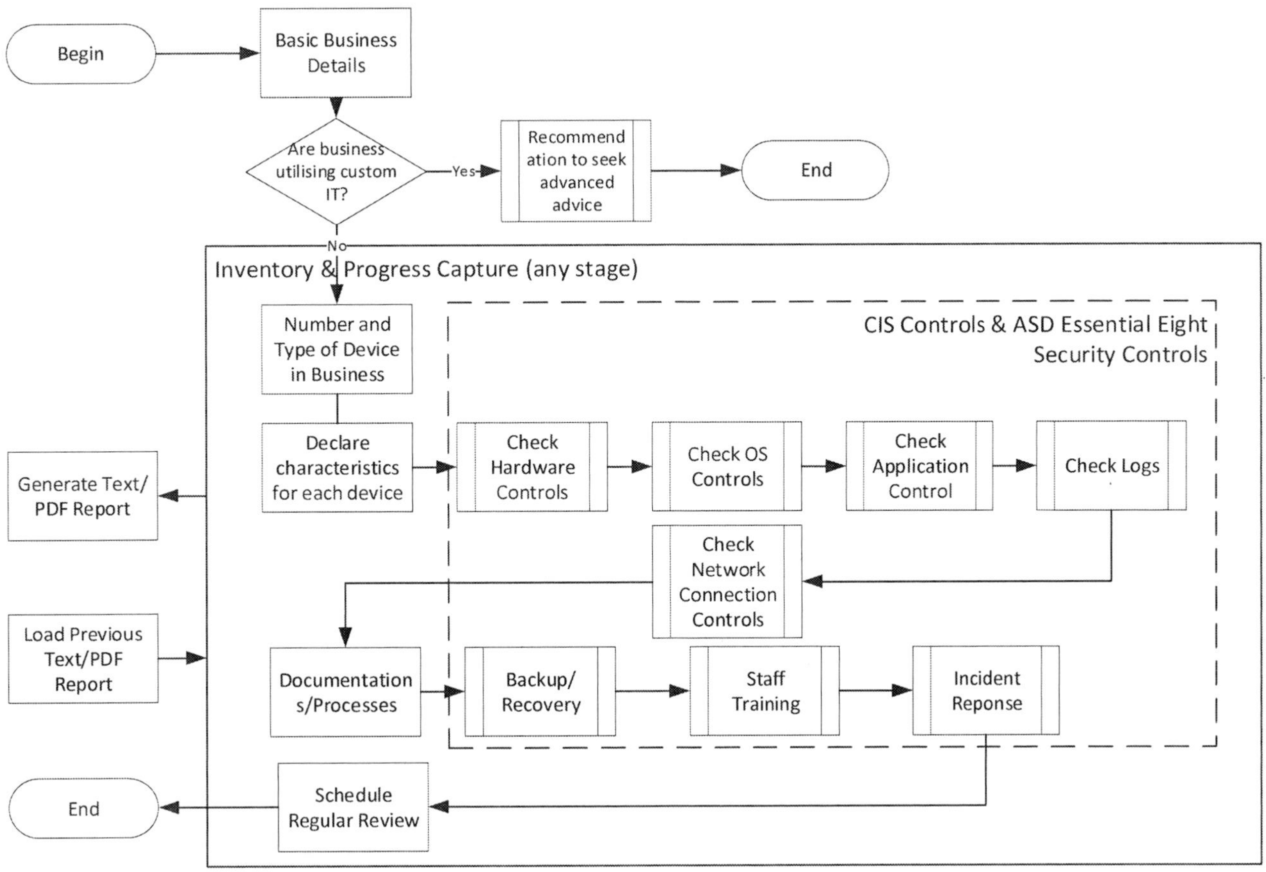

Fig. 2. Logic Flow of SE-CAP Questions for End Users: SE-CAP will first vet users for their suitability to use SE-CAP. Then SE-CAP collects information for the IT devices inventory. Collected device characteristics are used to display relevant instructions that helps users meet security controls from ASD Essential Eights and CIS Controls. The result of the process can be updated, paused and resumed via user save text/pdf reports. For detail description, see Section II-C

how to turn on automatic updates and/or apply updates manually. If the business operates a second Windows device, the information will be presented again for the second device. The repetition of advice for each device provides step by step clarity and focus for end users, and prevents logic jumps that may leave devices un-actioned.

3) Keeping Track: As the user completes each action, they are invited to note it in SE-CAP. They are given the options to skip actions at any time, e.g. enabling multi-factor authentication (MFA), for usability. Skipping allows scenarios where the device/action can't be completed immediately (e.g. a business is waiting for a software vendor's instructions on how to enable MFA). The lack of action will be noted in the output, and users will be reminded of the action(s) still to be completed when the process is resumed.

The relevant industry standard controls completed are noted in the output file, as the user goes through each section. This tracking facilitates a traceability of the effort that the business owner has invested into the process, thus providing a clear feedback loop [24] showing that their actions do have an impact on their vulnerability profile.

4) Pause Anytime: Users can pause and save via a local file export in a human-readable file, e.g. text, pdf etc, at any stage. When they are ready to resume the process, the same file is re-ingested into the website for editing. This record serves 2 main purposes:

- A saved file that a user can resume at a later stage.
- A business' IT inventory record and the cybersecurity state at a point in time. Both of these provide valuable information in future cybersecurity activities for internal and external stakeholders e.g. cybersecurity professionals.

This import/export function also allows business owners to easily update their existing inventory and security controls list.

5) A Continuous Process: Ideally, small business owners will complete SE-CAP in short sessions over multiple weeks. There are no limitations on the number of times and the length of time small business owners should spend on SE-CAP each time, allowing for flexibilities. For example, John, a small business owner, has a small window of time each Monday morning as he waits for a meeting to begin. John spends 15 minutes on SE-CAP and saves and resumes his progress over many weekly 15 minute sessions. Jane, on the other hand, suddenly had a 2 day training course cancelled. Jane can work through SE-CAP during those 2 days, exporting and resuming at the end of each day. In this case, SE-CAP would encourage Jane to schedule time slots in her calendar to revisit her answers.

The potential benefit of a repeated interaction model between SE-CAP and the user is the creation of an ongoing relationship and awareness of cybersecurity inside their business.

D. The Benefits of Self Assessment

SE-CAP's self-assessment model takes the opposite approach to the current cybersecurity industry model of individualised assessment. Self-assessment is a model that government and industry bodies have used to provide advice for other aspects of running a business e.g. licensing [11], food labeling [20] etc. A self-help approach is a valid strategy for small businesses, with the Australian Business Licensing Information Service (ABLIS) [11] (which connects business owners to disparate existing local licensing requirements and bodies) recording over 200,000 searches in the 2018-19 financial year [10].

SE-CAP's self-assessment deliberately places the tools within the hands of the business owner rather than the cybersecurity professional. The 2 main drivers for the self-assessment recommendations are:

- The reality that a cybersecurity professional is out of reach for small businesses, financially and logistically.
- The creation of a sense of self-efficacy and ownership of the security of their IT systems amongst small business owners.

The drive to raise self-efficacy is founded on established Protection Motivation Theory (PMT) research [27]; humans are more likely to take action to protect themselves if they feel that actions they take can lead to an effective outcome. Public health campaigns have successfully used PMT theories to promote individual actions for self protection [19] and information security is now starting to do the same [37], [25].

In SE-CAP, we promote self-efficacy by formulating questions based on IT concepts (i.e. devices) that small business owners are familiar with, thus clarifying the control that the small business has. The process further de-mystifies cybersecurity measures by linking the controls to tangible devices, thus increasing a sense of control and familiarity [27]. Encouraging protective behaviours encourages good cybersecurity habits from the small business owner themselves.

SE-CAP works well in a "working from home" scenario, as necessitated by COVID-19 restrictions in some countires. Work from home introduces the complexity of a delicate balance between privacy and thoroughness that many businesses of various sizes are working through.

By asking each employee to perform SE-CAP individually and reporting back on their level of compliance gives business owners the assurance that a certain level of security has been followed, while leaving the details of the employee's home IT setup relatively private.

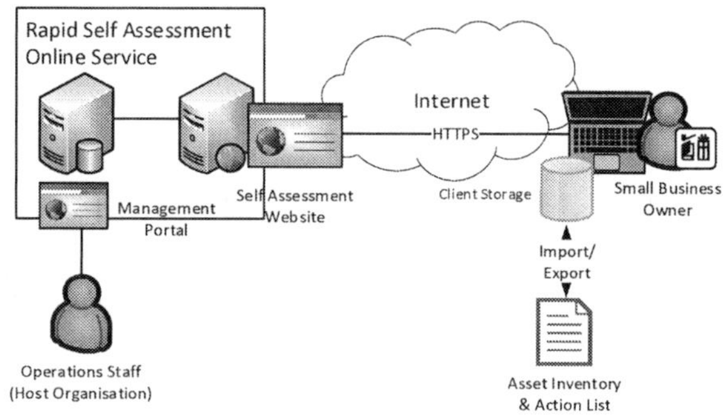

Fig. 3. Self Assessment System Reference Architecture: SE-CAP reference architecture contains only a handful of generic components. The main architecture blocks include web application, database, URL, internet and an internet enabled user device. These architecture blocks can be implemented using a variety of widely available technologies. See Section III for further details.

E. The Security Controls

The questions, the actions, and how these are presented hold the key to the usability of SE-CAP. To this end, the questionnaire in SE-CAP centers on language and objects that users are familiar with: device, Internet connection and business processes. The value of SE-CAP is in relating everyday business concepts back to established cybersecurity standards in a meaningful and measurable way.

The questions and control actions are initially based on two established cybersecurity standards: CIS Control [13] and the Australian Signal Directorate's (ASD) Essential Eight [8]. These standards are chosen for:

- Device centric approach,
- Incremental process starting from small actions,
- Traceability and clear migration path into a comprehensive security standard.

A clear migration path to a comprehensive standard is critical to a business' journey, as cybersecurity readiness is a continuous process. These 2 standards provide a path, when the need arises, to further develop a small business' security posture.

CIS Control and ASD Essential Eight's control points are separated into device, network connections and process categories for SE-CAP. In SE-CAP the control points do not follow the sequence given in either standard, as neither standard claims any strict order dependency. When the output document is exported, the user is shown a list of control points that have been fulfilled and not fulfilled from each standard.

III. System Architecture

SE-CAP intentionally uses generic web technologies to increase a host organisation's ability to deploy and maintain. SE-CAP's reference architecture as described in Figure 3.

SE-CAP can be developed in any programming language that supports client-side data, server-side database, web-forms and basic logic. At a high level, SE-CAP is a web application attached to a database. This web application is made available, via web front-end servers, to the Internet. End user access is via an advertised URL (over HTTPs for secure data carriage).

Generic assessment information is served from the server to the client to enable the display of pages. The bulk of the business specific data, i.e. what the user inputs, are confined to the client-side for security purposes.

Note that the precise technology to employ will depend on the technology stack and capability of the host organisation. All mentions of specific technologies are merely an example, and the best option must be chosen to suit the target hosting environments.

A. Client Side Technology

One noted architectural difference between SE-CAP and a common website is the heavy reliance on client-side storage. The client data storage serves as additional privacy protection, in addition to the HTTPs connectivity, to minimise transit of sensitive business data over unsecured networks. This also minimises the sensitive data to be stored and dealt with by the server. All persistent data is stored on the client-side only, see Figure 4. The persistent client data gets exported as a local file that the small business owner retains.

The client-side storage of data, using technology such as IndexedDB [36], Cache Storage API [28] etc, prevents transmission of sensitive data across potentially untrusted network connections. The information sent from server to client is at a high level and does not include precise details of business specific devices/processes.

The implementation of a client-side heavy design is an unconventional architectural decision, which has associated challenges that will be discussed in Section IV-A.

B. Inventory/Progress File

The data saving mechanism as an output of the self-assessment is intended to be a record for the small business. This is provided in the form of client-side text file export libraries e.g. jsPDF [29]. The client-side libraries are recommended to address the data storage and security risks associated. At no stage are the servers expected to process or save the data that business owners input.

Regardless of implementation technology, the import/export files must:

- Be human readable, serving both as a saved file and a business record,
- Contain progress of questions, actions and references completed and outstanding,
- Contain referenced security controls that have been marked as completed.

By serving multiple purposes, SE-CAP allows for easier maintenance and a smaller footprint.

C. Management Portal

Another important aspect of SE-CAP is the management interface of the database. This allows the database to be updated with changes to any aspects of the security controls and associated data. The changes will then allow the latest external references to be presented to small business owners, ensuring ongoing relevance of the advice. The rapidly changing nature of IT and cybersecurity means that a dedicated management portal on SE-CAP for the operational staff to change this information is required. Requiring code update on the website to change minor details such as links is not practicable for the long term viability of SE-CAP.

D. Real (or Near Real) Time Support

To further increase the self-efficacy of the user, optional live support functions can be deployed using many existing technologies, ranging from live chats, peer support forums to ticket based systems. While not a core function, the ability to assist users would be beneficial in both helping users and being able to receive feedback on how SE-CAP can be improved. Existing psychological theory [33] points to the role that supportive relationships can play in changing behaviour. For many business owners, especially non-technical users who may be undertaking cyber-security audits for the first time, this support can provide the encouragement to persist with this exerecise.

The choice of technology used to provide support to users will depend upon existing norm and conventions, within the host organisation.

IV. Challenges of Self-Assessment System

Despite technical flexibility and reuse of proven web technology, there are challenges to implementing SE-CAP. Some of these can be solved by an investment in architectural design and integration efforts. There are also several non-technical considerations that need further investigation.

A. Client Emphasis

Due to the unusual architecture of relying heavily on client-side web browser execution in both logic and data of SE-CAP, some features of server-side processing are not available. When deploying this solution, host organisations must consider the following aspects:

- Performance - The use of client-side logic places significant processing workload on the client-side browser. Depending on the expected computing power that the small business users are likely to have, a re-balancing between the amount of client-side processing and confidentiality of data may be required. It may be necessary to place certain business sensitive data back onto the server-side to alleviate client computing load.
- Data Validation - An advantage of server-side storage of data is the ability of the server to validate data passed in by a client. As server-side data validation is not possible in this solution, developers of the platform need to be mindful of the increased likelihood of faulty inputs from the client side and develop the system to handle and secure against these scenarios.

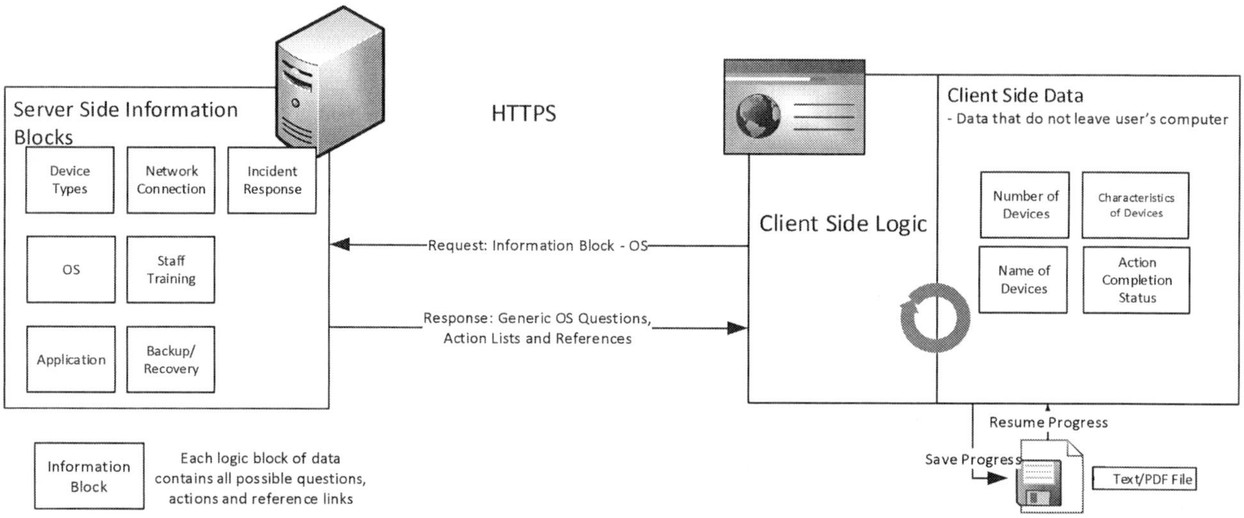

Fig. 4. High Level Server vs Client Data Storage and Data Interactions at a Software Level: The sensitive business data, in the ideal architecture, never leaves the client machine. Blocks of generic question are sent from the server, and processed on the client side for display. See Section 4 for further details.

B. Usability for Small Business Owners

The ability to use SE-CAP largely depends on small business owners being able to understand and answer the questions on their own. To enable this, all user related aspects of the system must be carefully crafted in language and functions familiar to a non-technical audience. While it is expedient to use the language within each relevant cybersecurity standard, this language is not understood by all business owners [9]. As an example, to address CIS Control 1.6 [13], SE-CAP can ask questions around whether there are any strange computers or phones in their router list of connections, rather than framing questions in terms of "unauthorised assets" as described in the control. At a terminology level, usability can also be enhanced by using specific terms such as "phone", "internet router", "laptop" etc. in place of an industry (but technically correct) term such as "device". A non-technical user is not likely to understand the underlying assumption that "device" encompass a variety of types of equipment.

The legibility of the language used is vitally important, as the primary audience of SE-CAP is unlikely to have the technical training or experience that cyber-security professionals have. At a practical level, one way of supporting the empowerment of small business owners is to conduct user experience design activities to ensure the appropriateness of the language used.

C. Gaps Between & In Cybersecurity Standards

Most cybersecurity standards do not cover all aspects of cybersecurity practices at a day to day level. One notable gap is around incident response: the actions required to be taken once a breach has occurred. Most advice has centred around prevention. Post-breach help in varied degrees that has been set up by governments worldwide [22], [23], mostly targets private individuals. Current advice is far from useful for small businesses, despite a small business' intertwined relationship with their owners. Our analysis for this solution proposal has identified a significant lack of official small business cybersecurity incident response measures.

Incident response advice needs to be included as part of SE-CAP. In the interim, the host organisation of SE-CAP, with a specific audience in mind, will be best placed to put together that advice. This custom advice is a short term remediation until a long term industry approach is developed.

Other gaps may be discovered within the standards during detailed security control and question mapping activities. Knowledge gaps will need to be filled by SE-CAP's host organisation on a case by case basis until a coordinated industry approach is found.

D. Legal Considerations

Due to the advisory nature of SE-CAP, its legal status will change depending upon SE-CAP's host entity. A few points which should be considered, from the host organisation's perspective are:

- Regulatory framework for business advice,
- Existing local laws around cyber crimes,
- Existing local processes and support around cyber crimes/identity theft,
- Host's relationship with the small business owner,
- Any specific industry regulations.

E. Host Organisation

In recent years, cyber-security has been debated in many contexts [34], [15] as a public good. Countries like Singapore now treat the cyber-security of its community similar to basics such as sanitation and product safety [14]. Cyber-security can no longer be considered a purely private good from an economic point of view. The support of small business cyber-security protects not just the small business owners, but also the data and identities of their customers and any associated entities.

As a tool that enables the delivery of a collective cyber-security good, it is imperative to recognise that there are multiple candidate host organisation(s) suitable for the hosting of SE-CAP, e.g. government deparments, industry associations or statutory bodies. Other than a host that can supply the technical resource and management requirements already discussed thus far, considerations from the perpective of best arranagement to provide cyber-security as a common/public service needs to be further studied. It is a topic that can greatly benefit from the learnings and lessons from the field of collective good/services policies [32].

V. Extendibility

SE-CAP can be expanded with the inclusion of further cybersecurity standards and specialisations. A particular industry may choose to add industry-specific questions and controls upon this base. By starting with the universal building blocks of cybersecurity in the users and IT devices, the data and question model can be extended to suit niche or specialised situations.

VI. Conclusion

We have proposed SE-CAP to deal with the current surge in small business online activities due to COVID19. A distributed and self-help system has the best chance of reaching a large audience due to the current lack of cybersecurity expertise and resources. By making cybersecurity approachable and achievable for even the least technical of business owners, SE-CAP has the potential to lift the cybersecurity posture of the small business cohort. The incremental improvement in security posture will benefit both small businesses and the cybersecurity industry, by limiting the number of "easy" targets that criminals can exploit. The limiting of the number of targets will eventually allow more focused investigation by law enforcement, and as a result better legal remediation potential for victims.

Acknowledgment

This research is supported by an Australian Government Research Training Program (RTP) Scholarship.

References

[1] R. J. Ackerman, "The Cyber Skills Shortage Continues to Balloon – and Think Tanks Aren't Helping," 2019. [Online]. Available: https://www.rsaconference.com/industry-topics/blog/the-cyber-skills-shortage-continues-to-balloon-and-think-tanks-arent-helping

[2] D. Almubayedh, M. A. Khalis, G. Alazman, M. Alabdali, R. Al-Refai, and N. Nagy, "Security Related Issues in Saudi Arabia Small Organizations: A Saudi Case Study," *21st Saudi Comput. Soc. Natl. Comput. Conf. NCC 2018*, pp. 1–6, 2018.

[3] D. Armstrong, "I Lost My Identity to a Fraudster, and It Took Six Years to Clean Up the Mess," Aug. 2019. [Online]. Available: https://www.bloomberg.com/news/articles/2019-08-12/i-lost-my-identity-to-a-fraudster-and-it-took-six-years-to-clean-up-the-mess

[4] AustCyber, "Australia's Cyber Security Sector Competitiveness Plan 2019 Update," 2019. [Online]. Available: https://www.austcyber.com/resource/australias-cyber-security-sector-competitiveness-plan-2019

[5] Australian Bureau of Statistics, "1321.0 - Small Business in Australia, 2001," 2001. [Online]. Available: https://www.abs.gov.au/ausstats/abs@.nsf/mf/1321.0

[6] ——, "8165.0 - Counts of Australian Businesses, including Entries and Exits, June 2014 to June 2018," 2019. [Online]. Available: https://www.abs.gov.au/AUSSTATS/abs@.nsf/DetailsPage/8165.0June2014toJune2018?OpenDocument

[7] ——, "8167 Selected Characteristics of Australian Business," 2019. [Online]. Available: https://www.abs.gov.au/AUSSTATS/abs@.nsf/allprimarymainfeatures/C575766838376FA0CA2573E1000E3F2F?opendocument

[8] Australian Cyber Security Centre, "Australian Signal Directorate Essential Eight Maturity Model," pp. 1–2, 2019. [Online]. Available: https://www.cyber.gov.au/node/100https://www.cyber.gov.au/publications/essential-eight-explained

[9] ——, "Supporting Small Businesses – The ACSC Small Business Cyber Security Guide and Companion Materials," Australian Cyber Security Centre, Tech. Rep., 2019.

[10] Australian Government, "ABLIS Analytics Dashboard," 2020. [Online]. Available: https://ablis.business.gov.au/reports

[11] ——, "Australian Business Licence and Information Service," 2020. [Online]. Available: https://ablis.business.gov.au/

[12] Australian Signals Directorate- Government of Australia, "Threat Update: COVID-19 malicious cyber activity," Australian Cyber Security Centre, Tech. Rep., 2020. [Online]. Available: https://www.cyber.gov.au/threats/threat-update-covid-19-malicious-cyber-activity-20-apr-2020

[13] Center for Internet Security, "CIS Controls," Center for Internet Security, Tech. Rep., 2019. [Online]. Available: www.cisecurity.org/controls/

[14] Cyber Security Agency of Singapore, "Our Organisation," 2020. [Online]. Available: https://www.csa.gov.sg/who-we-are/our-organisation

[15] Danilo D'Elia, "The Economics of Cybersecurity: From the Public Good to the Revenge of the Industry," in *Lect. Notes Comput. Sci. (including Subser. Lect. Notes Artif. Intell. Lect. Notes Bioinformatics)*, 2016, vol. 9588, pp. 3–15.

[16] Department of Parliamentary Services, "Small business sector contribution to the Australian economy," 2018. [Online]. Available: https://parlinfo.aph.gov.au/parlInfo/download/library/prspub/6272043/upload_binary/6272043.pdf

[17] V. Dimopoulos, S. Furnell, M. Jennex, and I. Kritharas, "Approaches to IT Security in Small and Medium Enterprises," in *Proc. 2nd Aust. Inf. Secur. Manag. Conf. Secur. Futur. Perth, West. Aust. Novemb. 26th, 2004*, 2004, pp. 73–82. [Online]. Available: https://www.researchgate.net/publication/221148270_Approaches_to_IT_Security_in_Small_and_Medium_Enterprises

[18] Eurostat, "ICT security in enterprises," 2020. [Online]. Available: https://ec.europa.eu/eurostat/statistics-explained/pdfscache/9132.pdf

[19] D. L. Floyd, S. Prentice-Dunn, and R. w. Rogers, "A Meta-Analysis of Research on Protection Motivation Theory," *J. Appl. Soc. Psychol.*, vol. 30, no. 2, pp. 407–429, 2000.

[20] Food Standards Australia New Zealand, "Nutrition Panel Calculator," 2019. [Online]. Available: https://www.foodstandards.gov.au/industry/npc/Pages/Nutrition-Panel-Calculator-introduction.aspx

[21] N. Gallagher, "One of KC's best craft cocktail bars adapts with bottled drinks and kits during coronavirus quarantine," *Kansas City Mag.*, Mar. 2020. [Online]. Available: https://www.kansascitymag.com/cocktail-hour-during-coronavirus-outbreak/

[22] IDCare, "IDCare," 2019. [Online]. Available: https://www.idcare.org

[23] JND Legal Administration, "Equifax Data Breach Settlement," 2020. [Online]. Available: https://www.equifaxbreachsettlement.com/en/amend

[24] K. A. Karl, A. M. O'Leary-Kelly, and J. J. Martocchio, "The Impact of Feedback and Self-Efficacy on Performance in Training," *J. Organ. Behav.*, vol. 14, no. 4, pp. 379–394, 1993.

[25] Y. Li, J. Wang, and H. R. Rao, "Adoption of identity protection service: An integrated protection motivation – precaution adoption process model," *AMCIS 2017 - Am. Conf. Inf. Syst. A Tradit. Innov.*, vol. 2017-Augus, pp. 1–9, 2017.

[26] J. Longbottom, "Coronavirus forces businesses to adapt to survive the COVID-19 pandemic," *ABC News*, Mar. 2020. [Online]. Available: https://www.abc.net.au/news/2020-03-19/how-businesses-adapting-to-survive-covid-19-coronavirus/12068696

[27] J. E. Maddux and R. W. Rogers, "Protection motivation and self-efficacy: A revised theory of fear appeals and attitude change," *J. Exp. Soc. Psychol.*, vol. 19, no. 5, pp. 469–479, 1983.

[28] Mozilla Developer Network, "CacheStorage," 2020. [Online]. Available: https://developer.mozilla.org/en-US/docs/Web/API/CacheStorage

[29] MrRio, "jsPDF Library," 2020. [Online]. Available: https://github.com/MrRio/jsPDF

[30] Organisation for Economic Co-operation and Development (OECD), "Productivity by industry," *Oecd Product. Indic. Compend.*, 2018.

[31] ——, "Survey of Adult Skills (PIAAC): Full selection of indicators," Paris, 2019. [Online]. Available: https://gpseducation.oecd.org/IndicatorExplorerhttps://doi-org.ezproxy.lib.rmit.edu.au/10.1787/eco_surveys-aus-2018-graph60-en.

[32] V. Ostrom and E. Ostrom, "Public Goods and Public Choices," in *Polycentricity Local Public Econ. Readings from Work. Polit. Theory Policy Anal.* University of Michigan Press, 1999, p. 75.

[33] J. Prochaska, C. Diclemente, and J. Norcross, "In Search of How People Change: Applications to Addictive Behaviors," *Am. Psychol.*, vol. 47, no. 9, pp. 1102–1114, 1992.

[34] M. Taddeo, "Is Cybersecurity a Public Good?" *Minds Mach.*, vol. 29, no. 3, pp. 349–354, 2019. [Online]. Available: https://doi.org/10.1007/s11023-019-09507-5

[35] U.S. Small Business Administration, "2019 Small Business Profile," U.S. Small Business Administration, Office of Advocacy, Tech. Rep., 2019. [Online]. Available: https://cdn.advocacy.sba.gov/wp-content/uploads/2019/04/23142719/2019-Small-Business-Profiles-US.pdf

[36] W3C, "Indexed Database API 2.0," 2018. [Online]. Available: https://www.w3.org/TR/IndexedDB-2/

[37] I. M. Woon, G. W. Tan, and R. T. Low, "A protection motivation theory approach to home wireless security," *Assoc. Inf. Syst. - 26th Int. Conf. Inf. Syst. ICIS 2005 Forever New Front.*, pp. 367–380, 2005.

Google/Apple Exposure Notification Due Diligence

Douglas J. Leith, Stephen Farrell
Trinity College Dublin, Ireland

Abstract—**We report on an independent assessment of the Android implementation of the Google/Apple Exposure Notification (GAEN) system. While many health authorities have committed to making the code for their contact tracing apps open source, these apps depend upon the GAEN API for their operation and this is not open source. Public documentation of the GAEN API is also limited. We find that the GAEN API uses a filtered Bluetooth LE signal strength measurement that can be potentially misleading with regard to the proximity between two handsets. We also find that the exposure duration values reported by the API are coarse grained and can somewhat overestimate the time that two handsets are in proximity. Updates to the GAEN API that can affect contact tracing performance, and so public health, are silently installed on user handsets. While facilitating rapid rollout of changes, the lack of transparency around this raises obvious concerns.**

I. Introduction

In early April 2020, Apple and Google formed a partnership to develop Covid-19 contact event detection based on Bluetooth LE [1]. Following public launch of the Google/Apple Exposure Notification (GAEN) API on 20 May [2], GAEN implementations are now installed on many people's phones and this API is starting to be used by national health authority contact tracing apps.

Even though many health authorities have committed to making the code for their contact tracing apps open source, these apps depend upon the GAEN API for their operation. The GAEN API is not open source and the public documentation [3] is limited. On Android the GAEN API is implemented within Google Play Services[1]. The GAEN implementation is silently installed without user opt-in on handsets running Google Play Services, although so far its functionality appears to be disabled until a Google approved app is installed that offers the user the choice to opt-in. It then subsequently also silently updates itself. There is almost no public information on the nature of updates (such as a changelog) nor notice of their release, and users running Google Play Services have no opt out from them.

This state of affairs would be undesirable for any software, but is especially so for software that is likely to be widely used in apps backed by national governments and health authorities and which may impact public health. Here we take a first step towards public "due diligence" of the GAEN API.

Using experimental measurements we assess the relationship between Bluetooth LE received signal strength (RSSI) and the attenuation duration values reported by the GAEN API. We find that the GAEN API uses a filtered RSSI value that can be potentially misleading with regard to the proximity between two handsets (it may suggest handsets are further apart than they really are)[2].

The GAEN API reports *exposure duration* (durationMinutes) and *attenuation duration*. The "exposure duration" terminology suggests that this value is an estimate of the aggregate time that two handsets are in close proximity, but in fact we find that this value is an estimate of the time during which a handset can see beacons from another handset, regardless of the distance between the two handsets.

Since the GAEN API only scans for Bluetooth LE beacons about every 4 mins, the reported exposure duration information is necessarily coarse-grained. Our measurements show that the reported duration values increase by a sequence of sharp jumps as time progresses and that the reported duration values may run ahead of clock time, e.g. a duration of 20 mins may be reported when the actual time that two handsets are in proximity is 15 mins.

When two handsets are only intermittently in proximity, e.g. when two handsets spend several 5 min intervals in close proximity but in between spend time apart, we find that periods apart of less than 10 mins apart may be missed by the API and treated as a single continuous exposure, thus

The authors would like to extend their thanks to the Irish HSE for arranging with Google for us to have whitelisted access to the GAEN API. We emphasise that any views expressed in this report are the authors own, and may not be shared by the HSE. Trinity College Dublin, (the authors' employer) funded the "Testing Apps for Contact Tracing" (TACT) project that has allowed us the time and handsets required for this work.

[1]The choice to implement the Android GAEN API within Google Play Services mandates the installation and use of Google Play Services in order to use contact tracing apps based on the API. Google Play Services is closed-source proprietary software that is used by many Google products. Coupling national contact tracing apps with Google Play Services therefore means that national governments are potentially being co-opted for the commercial benefit of Google. This warrants further analysis. Note also that due to this packaging choice and current US export controls, some handset manufacturers and countries may be prevented from using the GAEN API.

[2]Following discussions with Google on foot of the work reported here the GAEN documentation has now been updated to note that GAEN takes measurements only on channel 37 and also to include additional details on the calculation of attenuation level and duration consistent with the analysis reported here.

Workshop on Secure IT Technologies against COVID-19 (CoronaDef) 2021
21 February 2021, Virtual

https://dx.doi.org/10.14722/coronadef.2021.23005
www.ndss-symposium.org

overestimating the exposure time, e.g. two periods of 5 min exposure separated by 5 mins apart is reported as 20 mins exposure. We note that intermittent scanning generally means that changes in proximity that happen between scans cannot be detected.

It is not the inaccuracy or otherwise per se of these duration values that is the primary concern here. Rather it is the lack of information about the design decisions that have been made within the GAEN API, and the lack of open discussion/evaluation of the potential impact of these design decisions on contact tracing efficacy. Note that the GAEN design decisions that happen to have been made are not the only ones possible, other design choices are available. For example the GAEN API might scan more frequently when it detects other handsets nearby so as to obtain more fine-grained information on exposure time. Whether this is a good idea or not is of course unclear, the point is that open discussion and evaluation of the impact that choices such as these have on contact tracing and infection control is needed.

Similarly, while silent updating of the GAEN implementation by Google allows rapid rollout of any "fix", should a "fix" be needed, such updates can affect the performance of contact tracing apps based on the GAEN API, and so in turn affect public health. The lack of transparency around this raises obvious concerns.

II. Google/Apple Exposure Notification API

A. Hardware & Software Used

We used Google Pixel 2s running GAEN API version 202490002.We used a version of the Google exemplar Exposure Notification app modified to allow us to query the GAEN API over USB using a python script (the source code for the modified app is available on github [4]). In addition we also wrote our own GAENAdvertiser app that implements the transmitter side of the GAEN API.

B. Measuring Bluetooth RSSI

Bluetooth advertises beacons on three radio channels so as to improve tolerance of interference. Beacons are broadcast on each channel in turn. Each channel may have different radio propagation characteristics, and be subject to different levels of interference from other transmitters, and so beacons sent from different channels may be received with different signal strengths. This behaviour can be seen, for example, in Figure 1(a) which plots the RSSI values reported by the standard Android BluetoothLeScanner API[3] when two handsets are placed 1m apart in an indoor location. It can be seen that the reported RSSI values roughly hop between -82dB, -84dB and -87dB in a regular, repeating pattern. Figure 1(b) plots counts of the number of times that each RSSI value is reported over

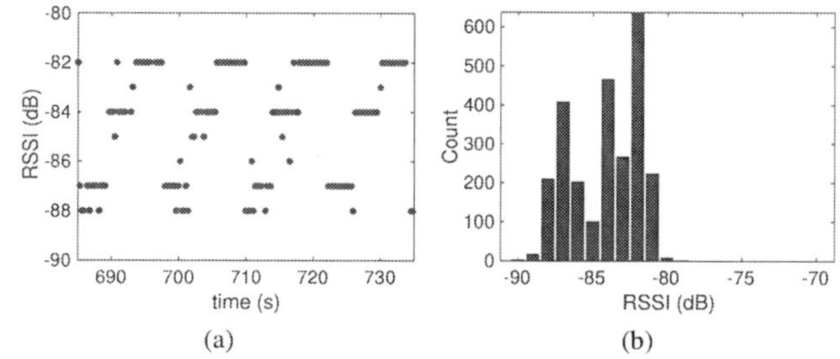

Fig. 1. Measured RSSI for two handsets placed 1m apart. (a) Snapshot of the corresponding RSSI time history, (b) histogram showing number of times each RSSI value is observed.

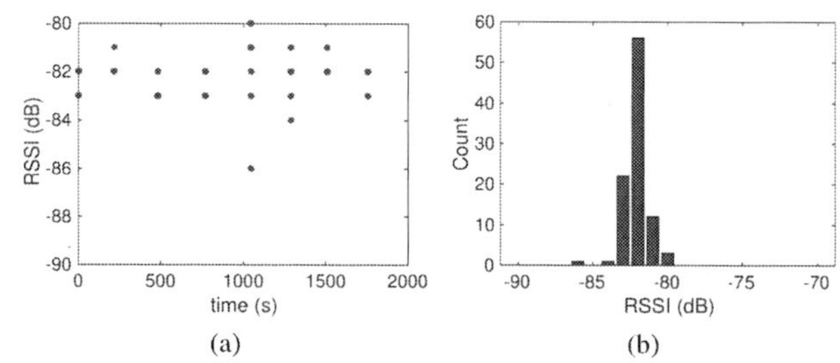

Fig. 2. RSSI values logged by GAEN API for two handsets placed 1m apart. Comparing (a) with Figure 1(a) it can be seen that the GAEN API focusses on the RSSI values around -82dB. This is also evident when comparing the histogram data in (b) with that in Figure 1(b) from which it can be seen the the GAEN API RSSI values correspond to the first peak at -82dB, with the other peaks having been filtered out.

a 20 minute period. Note the three peaks at -82dB, -84dB and -87dB, consistent with Figure 1(a).

Although we cannot see inside the GAEN API, on Android it does report RSSI values in the handset log. Figure 2 plots these values for the same setup at in Figure 1 (so these two figures can be directly compared). It can seen that the GAEN API RSSI values seem to correspond to beacons from only one channel, namely the channel corresponding to the -82dB peak in Figure 1(b). Similar behaviour is observed across a range of handset configurations and indicates that the GAEN API is carrying out filtering of the RSSI values (we will return to this later). One immediate implication of this is that some caution is needed if using RSSI values reported by the BluetoothLeScanner to estimate/predict performance of the GAEN API.

Also evident from Figure 2 is that the GAEN API only scans for beacons roughly every 250s (about 4 mins).

C. GAEN Attenuation Thresholds & Durations

The GAEN API does not report RSSI values but rather *attenuation durations* above/within/below *attenuation thresholds* that are specified when querying the API. We note that while the GAEN documentation was previously silent on how the attenuation thresholds relate to RSSI, following discussions with Google it has now been updated consistent with the analysis reported here.

[3]See https://developer.android.com/reference/android/bluetooth/le/BluetoothLeScanner. The scanner was configured to use SCAN_MODE_LOW_LATENCY so that it tries to report the RSSI of every beacon observed.

1) Attenuation: When we query the API we supply two attenuation thresholds A and B. The API then responds with three values:(i) the duration the attenuation was below A, (ii) the duration the attenuation was between A and B and (iii) the duration the attenuation was above B. For example we might choose A=48dB, B=63dB and obtain values 0, 10, 30 indicating no attenuation values below 48dB were observed, attenuation values between 48dB and 63dB were observed for a duration of 10 mins and attenuation values above 63dB were observed for 30 mins.

We can make repeated queries with different values of A and B. In particular, by holding A constant at a low value, e.g. 48dB, and then increasing B from 48dB to a high value, e.g. 100dB, in steps of 1 dB then we can extract fine-grained information on the durations at each attenuation value in the range 48dB to 100dB.

Figure 3(a) plots the attenuation value durations obtained using this repeated query approach for two handsets placed 1m apart. That is, corresponding to Figures 1 and 2. It can be seen that the attenuation values are tightly concentrated on 70dB whereas in Figure 2 the RSSI values are concentrated around -82dB. The "attenuation" terminology suggests that the attenuation value is given by the transmit power minus the RSSI, perhaps with some additional calibration for device specific characteristics. Supposing the transmit power to be -16dB (we will return to this shortly) then that suggests an attenuation value of 66dB. The handset log entries generated by the GAEN API suggest an offset of -4dB is added[4] to the RSSI to obtain a "calibrated RSSI". Adding this offset then suggests an attenuation value of 70dB, matching what we see in Figure 3(a).

The transmit power used in this attenuation calculation appears to be derived from the metadata included in GAEN beacons. We wrote an app that generates beacons according to the GAEN format and which allows us to specify the metadata sent in the beacons. Figure 3(b) plots the attenuation durations as the *transmit power level* value in the beacon metadata is varied from 0dB to 15dB for two handsets placed 1m apart. Note that in this plot we present the data using a coloured heatmap. We split the range of attenuation values shown on the y-axis into 2dB bins i.e. 70-72dB, 72-74dB and so on. Within each bin the colour indicates the percentage of the total reported duration that was spent in that bin, e.g bright green indicates that more than 90% of the time was spent in that bin. The mapping from colours to percentages is shown on the righthand side of the plot. Bins with no entries (i.e. with duration zero) are left blank. The solid line indicates the average attenuation level at each transmit power level (the average is calculated by weighting each attenuation level by the duration at that level and then summing over all attenuation levels).

[4]This value is dependent on the handset model, e.g. we observe that it is -4dB for Google Pixel 2s and -3dB for Samsung Galaxy A10s.

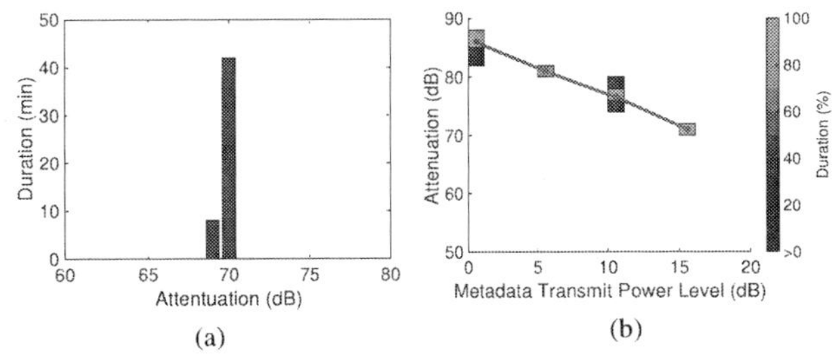

Fig. 3. Measured attenuation durations reported by the GAEN API vs time for two handsets placed 1m apart. (a) shows data corresponding to that in Figure 2, (b) shows the reported durations as the transmit power level value in the GAEN beacon metadata is varied from 0 to -15dB.

It can be seen from Figure 3(b) that the GAEN API reports that the attenuation durations are consistently concentrated in a single bin, as expected from Figure 3(a) (which is for the same physical setup). It can be seen that the attenuation value where the API reports most of the time being spent decreases linearly as the transmit power level sent in the beacon metadata is increased, as expected if the metadata transmit power value is being used in the attenuation calculation.

In these tests we used Google Pixel 2 handsets. The Android Bluetooth LE Advertiser API reports that the transmit power associated with advertising beacons at the TX_POWER_LOW setting is -16dB. When we use this metadata value in our app the attenuation durations reported by the GAEN API are essentially identical to those shown in Figure 3(a)[5].

In summary, by making repeated queries to the GAEN API we can obtain the reported duration value at each attenuation level. The attenuation value itself seems to be calculated as the $P_{TX} - P_{RX}$ where P_{TX} is the transmit power level sent in the beacon metadata and P_{RX} is given by the filtered RSSI plus a calibration value which is -4dB for the Google Pixel 2 handsets used in these tests.

2) Attenuation Duration: Figure 4(a) plots the total[6] reported attenuation duration vs time for two handsets placed 1m apart, i.e. the same setup as considered above. We queried the GAEN API regularly every minute and the solid line in Figure 4(a) shows the evolution of reported attenuation delay value over time. It can be seen that the attenuation duration increases in discrete jumps, rather than continuously, presumably reflecting the intermittent nature of the beacon scanning process noted previously. Also, that it can get ahead of clock time (this occurs when it lies above the dashed line marked in Figure 4(a)). For example, early in this test (well before 5mins clock time has elapsed) the attenuation is reported as being 5mins.

[5]Note that Google has since changed the transmit power level value sent in the beacon metadata in an attempt to compensate for differences in Bluetooth LE transmission characteristics between different models of handset. For example, in the most recent version of GAEN on Pixel 2s the transmit power level sent in the beacon metadata is now -31dB rather than -16dB. We highlight this as an example of a silently pushed update that has a substantial impact on the behaviour of contact tracing apps based one the GAEN API.

[6]The sum of the three attenuation duration values reported by the API.

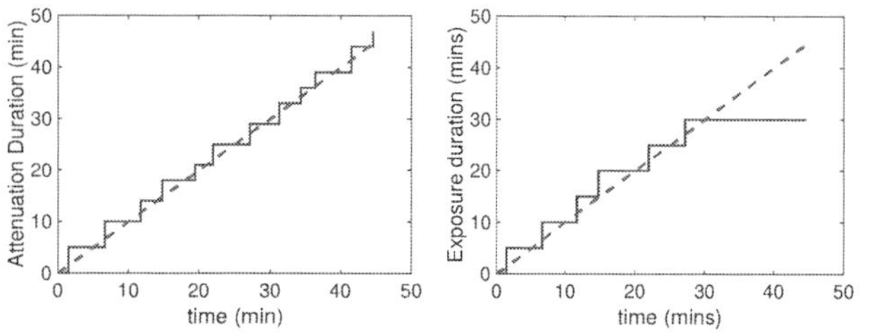

(a) Attenuation duration (b) Exposure duration

Fig. 4. Attenuation and exposure durations reported by the GAEN API vs time for two handsets placed 1m apart. The 45° line is indicated by dashes.

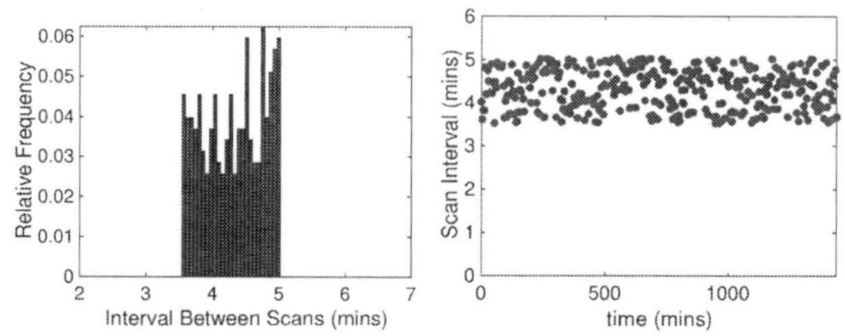

(a) (b)

Fig. 5. Measured intervals between GAEN API Bluetooth LE scans, based on 24 hours of data. (a) Relative frequency of scan intervals, (b) time history.

In Figure 4(a) the two handsets are in continuous proximity. We also collected measurements when are in proximity for 5 mins, separated for a variable period and then brought in proximity again for 5 mins (we simulated separating the handsets by disabling beacon transmission for a specified period). When the handsets are separated for 5 mins the API responds to a query with a single exposure information records that reports the attenuation duration 19 mins, suggesting that the GAEN API ignores the period when the handsets are separated. When the handsets are separated for 10 mins the API responds to a query with two exposure information records, the first reporting an attenuation duration on 5 mins and the second an attenuation duration of 10 mins. So although the aggregate attenuation duration of 15 mins is an overestimate (the actual time the handsets are together in only 10 mins) by responding with two exposure information records the API does seem to recognise that the handsets have been separated. When the handsets are separated for 15 mins the API response with two exposure information records each reporting an exposure duration of 5 mins, i.e. 10 mins in total.

In summary, the attenuation duration value seems to roughly track clock time, in line with the GAEN API documentation [3]. Intermittent handset proximity can be roughly inferred from the number of exposure information records with which the API responds.

D. GAEN Exposure Duration

The GAEN API reports an *exposure duration* value, but the documentation [3] says little about how this value is calculated beyond the fact that its value is given in units of 5 mins,.

Figure 4(b) plots the exposure duration reported by the GAEN API vs time when two handsets are placed 1m apart. We queried the GAEN API regularly every minute and the solid line in Figure 4(b) shows the evolution of reported exposure duration value over time. It can be seen that the exposure duration increases in 5 min jumps. Also, that it is frequently ahead of clock time (this occurs when it lies above the dashed line marked in Figure 4(b)) and is capped at 30 mins.

The terminology "exposure duration" may suggest that the reported value only counts the time when two handsets are in proximity e.g. when the attenuation is below one of the thresholds specified when querying the API or when handsets are less than 2m apart. However, we observed the reported exposure duration value to be the same regardless of the thresholds specified and that the exposure duration value reports time spent when handsets are 4m apart. It therefore seems more appropriate to interpret the reported exposure duration value as the time during which two handsets are in close enough proximity for one to observe the Bluetooth beacons of the other, regardless of the received signal strength. Note that Bluetooth LE beacons typically have a range of 5-10m (and potentially further for devices using the newer Bluetooth LE v5.0).

Similarly to Section II-C2 we also observed the reported exposure duration when two handsets are in proximity for 5 mins, separated for a variable period and then brought in proximity again for 5 mins. When the handsets are separated for 5 mins the API responds to our query with a single exposure information record that reports an exposure duration is 20 mins. When they are separated by 10 mins the API responds to our query with two exposure information records, one reporting an exposure duration of 5 mins and the second reporting an exposure duration of 10 mins. So, once again, although the aggregate exposure duration of 15 mins is an overestimate, by responding with two exposure information records the API seems to recognise that the handsets have been separated. When the handsets are separated for 15 mins the API response with two exposure information records each reporting an attenuation duration of 5 mins, i.e. 10 mins in total.

In summary, the exposure duration value reported by the GAEN API seems to roughly track the aggregate time during which a handset can see beacons from another handset, regardless of the distance between the two handsets. Intermittent handset proximity can be roughly inferred from the number of exposure information records with which the API responds.

E. Scanning Frequency

The GAEN API scans intermittently for beacons. We left two handsets beside one another for 24 hours and using the GAE log reports recorded the intervals between scans for Bluetooth LE beacons. Figure 5 shows the relative frequency of the interval between scans. It can be seen from Figure 5(a) that

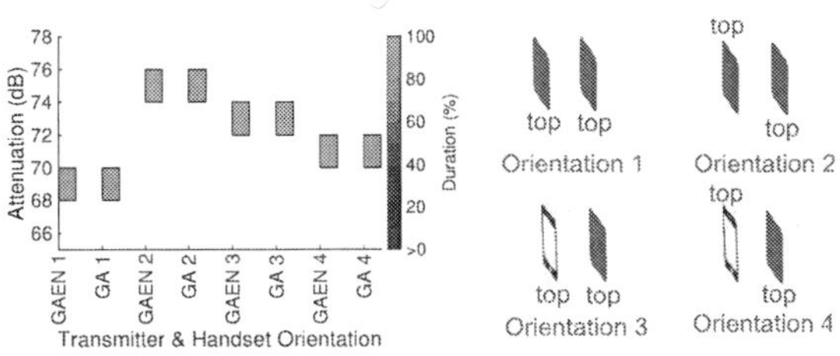

(a) (b)

Fig. 6. Attenuation durations reported by GAEN API for two Google Pixel 2 handsets placed 0.5m apart. One handset runs both the GAEN API and the GAENAdvertiser app and its orientation is changed as shown in (b). The x-axis labels indicate the transmitter (GAEN and GA, respectively) and the handset orientation for each GAEN report.

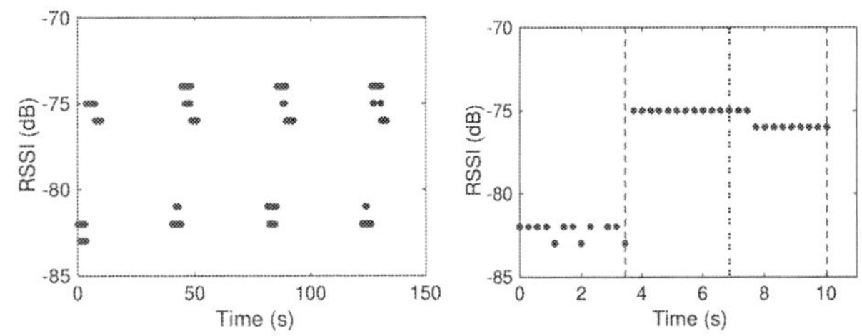

(a) (b)

Fig. 7. RSSI measurements reported by the standard Android Bluetooth scanner API when it is periodically (roughly every 30s) switched on, the first 36 RSSI values reported logged and then scanning halted. (b) is a zoomed-in view of the first set of RSSI measurements in (a). This data is for two Google Pixel 2's positioned 0.5m apart.

the scan intervals are roughly uniformly distributed between 3.5 mins and 5mins and from the time history in Figure 5(b) that the distribution of scan intervals is roughly constant over time (it does not, for example, increase overnight to reduce battery drain).

F. Inter-operability of GAEN Beacons

The GAEN API documentation [3] specifies the format of the Bluetooth LE beacons and the cryptographic protocol used to generate the payload of each beacon. To verify compliance of the Google Android GAEN API implementation with the specification, and to confirm inter-operability, we wrote the GAENAdvertiser app that generates beacons that follow the Bluetooth LE beacon protocol specified in the documentation.

This highlighted two lacuna's in the API documentation. Firstly, AES-CTR encryption is specified for the beacon metadata, but it is not stated when the counter used in this encryption is initialised. Our tests indicate that it is initialised when the first RPI is sent, and then incremented each time the RPI changes. Secondly, it is not stated how the metadata transmit power level value should be chosen. As discussed above, our measurements indicate that in fact this value is used by the GAEN API to calculate the attenuation level and so plays a key role in its operation.

Figure 6 shows example measurements comparing the reports generated by the GAEN API when it receives beacons generated by the GAEN API and beacons are generated by our GAENAdvertiser app (both running on the same handset to remove any other differences). This data is for two Pixel 2 handsets placed 0.5 apart. The relative orientation of the handsets is changed as shown schematically in Figure 6(b) and the GAEN API on one handset queried. Figure 6(a) shows the attenuation durations reported by the GAEN API in response to these queries for each orientation and for both the GAEN API on the second handset and the GAENAdvertiser app (labeled GAEN and GA respectively on the x-axis of Figure 6(a)). It can be seen that the reports are identical for the GAEN API and GAENAdvertiser beacons, and we also see similar behaviour in other measurements.

GAENAdvertiser is open source and can be obtained by contacting the authors. However, we have not made it publicly available since it can be used to faciltate a known replay attack against the GAEN API [5].

G. MAC Address Randomisation

The GAEN documentation specifies that Bluetooth LE beacon MAC address randomisation should be used when available, and that when the beacon content periodically changes the MAC address should also change so as to prevent linking of beacons from the same handset. In our measurements we observed that the GAEN API respected this behaviour.

III. GAEN RSSI FILTERING

In this section we take another look at the RSSI values which the GAEN API reports in the handset log. Recall that the attenuation durations reported by the API in response to queries seem to effectively be derived from these RSSI values.

We start by looking at the standard Android BluetoothLE scanner. The relevant code for this is also closed source, but we can deduce some aspects of its operation from Figure 7. This figure shows the RSSI values reported by the Android BluetoothLE scanner API when it is periodically (roughly every 30s) switched on, the first 36 RSSI values reported logged and then scanning halted. The beacons in this example are generated by a second handset running the GAEN API and located 0.5m away, but the behaviour is not specific to this. The scanner is configured to use SCAN_MODE_LOW_LATENCY, and so it tries to report on every beacon observed.

It can be seen from Figure 7(a) that the RSSI values reported by the scanner follow a regular pattern. Figure 7(b) shows a zoomed-in plot of the first set of samples, the vertical lines marking every 12 readings. Recall that Bluetooth LE transmits beacons on three separate radio channels, and so the scanner needs to listen to each of these three channels. What appears to be happening is that the scanner listens to one channel for a period of time (around 3s, corresponding to 12 beacons sent at 250ms intervals), then switches the next channel and listens to that for a period time (again, around 3s), then switches to the third channel. Since the channels are at different radio frequencies they have different signal propagation between the two handsets and so different RSSI values. Hence, as the scanner hops between the three channels we see jumps in the RSSI values roughly every 3s or 12 beacons. If we configure the scanner to collect more than 36 beacons then this pattern of RSSI jumps appears to repeat, with a switch back to values around -82dB for the next 12 beacons after the 36th beacon.

This behaviour is not especially interesting in itself, but is relevant to the GAEN API and Bluetooth LE contact detection for at least two reasons.

A. GAEN Effectively Monitors Only One Channel

Firstly, it means that it is likely that the GAEN API only listens to one out of the three channels that Bluetooth LE uses for transmitting beacons.

As can be seen from Figure 7(a) when first switched on the scanner always starts at the same channel (the one with RSSI around -82dB in this example). The channel hopping part of the scanner functionality is managed internally within Android, likely within the Bluetooth hardware driver[7]. That means it is also likely shared by the GAEN API. Based on the entries that it writes to the handset log the GAEN API scans for beacons periodically, around every 4 mins, and records the RSSIs for around 12 beacons. With Figure 7 in mind this suggests that the GAEN API collects RSSI values for only one of the three channels that Bluetooth LE uses for transmitting beacons. This is also consistent with the behaviour previously noted in Figure 2, and the observation that the GAEN RSSI values seem to correspond to only one of the three peaks in Figure 1(a).

B. Which Channel to Choose?

Collecting RSSI values for only one channel is potentially appealing as it removes the "noise" caused by hopping between channels, e.g the "smoother" nature of the values in Figure 2(a) compared to those in Figure 1(a) is immediately apparent. However, it can have some unwanted side effects.

Comparing again Figure 2(a) with Figure 1(a), it can be seen that the channel monitored by the GAEN API has the highest RSSI of the three channels at -82dB. However, this need not always be the case. For example in Figure 7 the channel that the scanner listens to first has the *lowest* RSSI of the three channels and so can potentially give a misleading view of proximity to the second handset, namely suggesting that the handset is further away than it really is.

This concern is not a hypothetical one. Figure 8 plots measurements taken on two Google Pixel 2 handsets placed 0.5m apart as their relative orientation is varied. The handsets are placed vertically, as illustrated schematically in Figure 6(b). The left-hand handset is rotated and flipped through each of the orientations shown in Figure 6(b) in turn. In this schematic

[7]Note that this means that the behaviour may change with the wireless chipset used in a phone. We used Google Pixel 2's on our tests but also see similar behaviour on a Samsung Galaxy A10 and a Huawei P10.

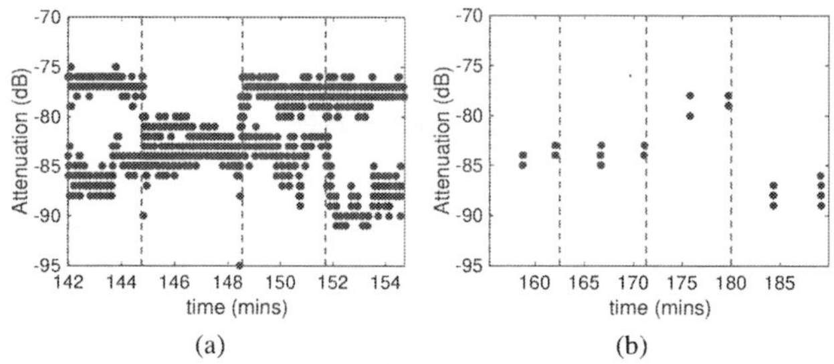

Fig. 8. Measurements taken on two Google Pixel 2 handsets placed 0.5m apart as their relative orientation is varied as shown schematically in Figure 6(b). In (a) the RSSI values are measured using the standard Android Bluetooth LE scanner, while in (b) the values are those written to the handset log by the GAEN API.

the top of the handsets is indicated, and the back of a handset is indicated as shaded. For example, in orientation 1 both the both handsets are top down with the screen facing to the right. In orientation 4 the left-hand handset is bottom down with the screen facing left, and so on.

In Figure 8(a) RSSI measurements from the standard Android Bluetooth LE scanner API are plotted as the orientation of the left-hand handset is changed. The vertical dashed lines indicate the times when the orientation changes. It can be seen that the changes in relative orientation change the RSSI, and in particular the spread of RSSI values across the three channels. For example, for the first orientation from time 142-144mins the RSSIs are divided into two bands, one around -87dB and another around -77dB, but for the second orientation from 144-148mins the RSSI/attenuations are bunched around -84dB.

Figure 8(b) shows the RSSI values logged by the GAEN API when the same experiment is repeated. It can be seen that for the first orientation the GAEN API uses RSSI values from the lower -85dB band rather than the higher -77dB band, whereas for the third orientation the GAEN API uses RSSI values from the higher 77dB band rather than the lower -84dB band that can be seen in the third section of Figure 8(a). For the last orientation the GAEN API uses RSSI values from the lower -87dB band in Figure 8(a) rather than the higher -77dB band.

IV. Summary and Conclusions

We first note that from an architectural perspective Google and Apple are today probably well placed to handle the kinds of issue noted here and to provide a "fix" that gets widely deployed, should a "fix" be needed. However, silently shipped changes to closed-source proprietary GAEN implementations can affect the performance of public health contact tracing apps based on the GAEN API, e.g. affecting the rate of exposure detection false positives and false negatives. The lack of transparency around this raises obvious concerns and reduces the value of health authorities and other app implementers making their client code publicly available.

References

[1] "Apple and Google partner on COVID-19 contact tracing technology," 10 April, 2020. [Online]. Available: https://www.apple.com/newsroom/2020/04/apple-and-google-partner-on-covid-19-contact-tracing-technology/

[2] Google Blog, "Exposure Notification API launches to support public health agencies," Accessed 13 June 2020. [Online]. Available: https://blog.google/inside-google/company-announcements/apple-google-exposure-notification-api-launches/

[3] "Exposure Notifications: Android API Documentation," accessed 6 June 2020. [Online]. Available: https://static.googleusercontent.com/media/www.google.com/en//covid19/exposurenotifications/pdfs/Android-Exposure-Notification-API-documentation-v1.3.2.pdf

[4] anon, "Modified Exposure Notification App," 9 June 2020. [Online]. Available: https://github.com/anon/BLEapp

[5] S. Farrell and D. Leith, "A Coronavirus Contact Tracing App Replay Attack with Estimated Amplification Factors," 19 May 2020. [Online]. Available: https://down.dsg.cs.tcd.ie/tact/replay.pdf

Differentially Private Health Tokens for Estimating COVID-19 Risk

David Butler*†, Chris Hicks*†, James Bell†, Carsten Maple†‡ and Jon Crowcroft†§
Email: {dbutler, chicks, jbell, cmaple, jcrowcroft}@turing.ac.uk
†Alan Turing Institute, ‡Univerity of Warwick, §University of Cambridge

Abstract—**In the fight against Covid-19, many governments and businesses are in the process of evaluating, trialling and even implementing so-called immunity passports. Also known as antibody or health certificates, there is a clear demand for any technology that could allow people to return to work and other crowded places without placing others at risk. One of the major criticisms of such systems is that they could be misused to unfairly discriminate against those without immunity, allowing the formation of an 'immuno-privileged' class of people. In this work we are motivated to explore an alternative technical solution that is non-discriminatory by design. In particular we propose health tokens — randomised health certificates which, using methods from differential privacy, allow individual test results to be randomised whilst still allowing useful aggregate risk estimates to be calculated. We show that health tokens could mitigate immunity-based discrimination whilst still presenting a viable mechanism for estimating the collective transmission risk posed by small groups of users. We evaluate the viability of our approach in the context of *identity-free* and *identity-binding* use cases and then consider a number of possible attacks. Our experimental results show that for groups of size 500 or more, the error associated with our method can be as low as 0.03 on average and thus the aggregated results can be useful in a number of *identity-free* contexts. Finally, we present the results of our open-source prototype which demonstrates the practicality of our solution.**

I. Introduction

The discussion surrounding immunity, antibodies and transmission risk have become synonymous with the fight against COVID-19. One technique that has been proposed is to certify each individuals' immunity status in a so-called immunity-passport. Because immunity to COVID-19 is not well understood, and the correlates to protection have not been fully identified, it has been proposed that these certificates (which are currently based on antibody testing) should be called antibody certificates [9].

Workshop on Secure IT Technologies against COVID-19 (CoronaDef) 2021
21 February 2021, Virtual

https://dx.doi.org/10.14722/coronadef.2021.23006
www.ndss-symposium.org

A number of antibody certificate solutions have already been proposed [2], [7], [10], [5], [9] and there has been significant discussion of the technical, social and ethical implications of the technology [12], [1], [13]. One of the main concerns relating to antibody certificates is that they could be misused to unfairly discriminate against people with respect to their immunity status. It has been suggested [9] that antibody certificates should not restrict peoples access to services, or freedom of travel, but could instead be useful as a tool for measuring aggregate transmission risk levels. To this end we approach this work with two assumptions in mind:

1) Immunity status is an attribute that should not be a basis for widespread, arbitrary discrimination.
2) It is useful to know the ratio (or count) of *immune* vs *non-immune* people that have accessed a service over a period of time — for example customers in a shop over a number of hours.

Our first assumption is motivated by concerns that immunity-based discrimination could threaten freedom, fairness and public health [13]. Particularly in the absence of a widely-available and effective vaccine: access to shops, transportation, religious establishments and medical services should perhaps not depend on whether wealth or luck has favoured an individual with immunity. We are motivated by these concerns to develop a system that technically mitigates immunity-based discrimination, using differential privacy, and to explore the limitations and practicality of our approach. Our second assumption is motivated by the idea that the presence and proximity of immune individuals may offer a proxy for estimating the risk of infection to those who are still susceptible [8].

Within the framework of these two assumptions we develop the idea of a *health token*: a randomised health certificate that allows the collective transmission risk[1] posed by groups of users to be estimated whilst also protecting individuals from immunity-based discrimination. Unlike previous work on antibody certificates, randomised health tokens are less likely to be used to

[1] We assume that a measure of transmission risk exists and that it can be accurately determined.

restrict access to services or transportation due to the uncertainty introduced in their true value. To achieve this we use the well known differential privacy technique of randomised response. Health tokens provide each user with a transmission risk that is plausibly deniable. Consequently, there is minimal incentive for user fraud and so the need to bind each user to their token is greatly diminished. Our health tokens comprise only a digitally signed, differentially private transmission risk status that allows aggregate transmission risk statistics to be computed.

In our proposed system, the transmission risk of each user is first evaluated by a healthcare provider who then cryptographically signs and issues the user a health token. Our system is independent of how this transmission risk is calculated and can support any number of different risk profiles, for example a scale of 1 to k. At present, we envisage the transmission risk being calculated through an antibody test, however note that other factors, like self reported symptoms, could also be considered.

Like many technology-based approaches to mitigating COVID-19, the effectiveness of health tokens is dependant on the number of people willing to participate in the system voluntarily. We envisage that, like digital contact tracing apps, citizens will be motivated to use health tokens by their will to bring social distancing measures to an end and to help in the fight against the disease.

In addition, our proposal may encourage users who would be reluctant to engage with a regular immunity-passport system that binds them directly to a certificate. Indeed our health tokens do not reveal any personal information, such as a name or photograph, which could either be used to trace a user across multiple contexts or be otherwise mishandled. Moreover the non-binding nature of our system means there is little risk of feature creep.

In Section II we detail our proposed system and in Section III we consider two types of use case: *identity-free* cases such as shops and *identity-binding* cases such as aeroplane flight booking. We consider and analyse some possible attacks on our system in Section IV. Finally in Section V we discuss the practicalities and limitations of our approach and in Section VI we review the related work and conclude.

II. Non Discriminatory Token System

Our system consists of three phases: issue, check and aggregate. In the issue phase a healthcare provider assesses the transmission risk of a user and then issues them with a cryptographically signed health token. In the check phase the service provider records the value of the users' health token. Finally, the aggregate phase allows the service provider to reconstruct the overall transmission risk associated with the 'checked' tokens.

A. The Health Token System

Here we present the three phases of our system in turn. First we denote the three stakeholders as follows: the healthcare provider Henry (H), the user Alice (A) and the service provider Verity (V, alliterative for verifier). Let $protocol_{DP}$ denote the differential privacy protocol that we use to compute our health tokens, then the three phases of our system are as follows:

Issue

1) H assesses A's transmission risk indicator to be $i_{true} \in \{0, \ldots, k-1\}$.
2) H computes $i_{rand} \leftarrow protocol_{DP}(i_{true}, \epsilon)$ and produces $token = \{i_{rand}, date_{issue}, date_{end}\}_{sgn_H}$ for A. Here $date_{issue}$ is the date the certificate is issued and $date_{end}$ is the date the token is no longer valid.
3) A receives i_{true} and $token$.

Check

1) A presents $\{token\}_{sgn_H}$ to V before accessing a service.
2) V verifies the signature and records the value $token$.

Aggregate

1) V finds the frequency, f, of each element of $\{0, \ldots, k-1\}$ amongst the $tokens$ it has received.
2) V debiases the frequency estimates as per Equation 1 to get an unbiased estimate of the the sum of the health tokens it has collected.

Each token is cryptographically signed by H. In particular we denote by $\{token, date_{issue}, date_{end}\}_{sgn_H}$ the user token, issue date and validity end date, signed with H's private signing key sgn_H. The bitstring representation of each signature will be unique (except for a negligible probability) for each token thus can be used as an identifier for each health token. We denote this identifier by *TID* — token identification number. Note that regardless of the user token value, A learns their true transmission risk. We include issue date and end date to indicate the freshness of the token and aid with revocation and the update of tokens. We discuss the updating of tokens at the end of this section.

B. The Differential Privacy Protocol

We use the differential privacy technique of randomised response [17] to produce a token based on the transmission risk of a user as evaluated by a healthcare provider. Informally, the protocol which we denote $protocol_{DP}$ is as follows.

The input is the users' true risk status $i_{true} \in \{0, \ldots, k-1\}$, which can be one of k options, and ϵ. Here, ϵ is a measure of the trade-off between privacy and accuracy; a low value of epsilon provides high privacy, but low utility (as the underlying distribution is more random) and vice versa. The protocol outputs i_{true} with probability $\frac{e^{\epsilon}-1}{e^{\epsilon}+k-1}$, else we select a uniformly random response from $\{0,\ldots,k-1\}$. Clearly it is possible to select a response at random and to still end up providing the true value.

An unbiased estimate $\hat{f}$ of the frequency f of a given option is calculated by putting the frequency it is returned as a response, $\tilde{f}$, into the following formula:

$$\hat{f} = \frac{e^{\epsilon}+k-1}{e^{\epsilon}-1}(\tilde{f}-1/k). \quad (1)$$

Error in re-aggregating the data is, of course, introduced with such a method. We visualise this error in our experiments in Section VI.

C. Update of tokens

It is important to consider the method, and effect of a user updating their health token. We assume that a users decision to get retested is independent of the randomness of their current token and that a user always uses the most recent certificate that has been issued to them. We advocate for short validity periods for certificates (for example two weeks). If a user does not get tested again within the validity period, their certificate (with the same token value) gets reissued to them automatically with extended end date. If the user is retested, a new certificate is issued to them, with new randomness introduced. Such an updating process allows for a simple and effective revocation system. The system is not perfect as, if retested, a user could hold more than one certificate at one time, however the old certificate will only be valid until its end date. Note the *TID* allows for the correct certificate to be re-issued in the case where a user holds more than one certificate.

III. Use Cases

Here we first give an example use case of our system, specifically we show how a shop could implement a risk analysis using health tokens. We then discuss the situations we do not think health tokens are appropriate; we conclude that health tokens are only suitable for *identity free* use cases.

Identity-Free Use Case – Allowing users into a shop: We consider a shop that wants to monitor the level of transmission risk inside at any given time. We construct a rudimentary risk model that demonstrates how our system could add benefit.

Let R be the natural number that represents the upper bound on acceptable risk in a shop at any one time and let T be the set of health tokens associated to people currently in the shop. Then

$$r = \sum_{t \in T} t$$

is a measure of the total transmission risk in the shop. We let t_n and t_e denote the token value of the next customer (in the queue to enter) and the exiting customer (the next customer to exit the shop). The next customer is let if and only if $r - i_e + i_n \leq R$.

Moreover it may be beneficial to aggregate the cumulative level of risk the shop has been exposed to over the course of a day or week — this may help guide when cleaning is most required, for example.

We reiterate that the risk model we have presented here is primitive. The method however could be abstracted to any risk model that is based on the customers token value. For example, it could take into account the size of the shop, the current staffing levels, the current spatial distribution of customers in the shop as well as the *freshness* of each certificate collected.

The example above suggests the utility of health tokens in adding a net positive benefit to society. Comparable uses could be monitoring the risk of crowds at sports stadiums and classes in schools.

Limits on Use Cases - Identity-Binding: We identify that not all situations are suitable for health tokens. Consider the example of filling seats on an aeroplane based on transmission risk. The objective function is ill-defined however the airline would likely want to limit risk while also filling as many seats as possible.

One can imagine a process where at the time of check-in, a passenger must also submit their health token value and the airline computes an aggregated risk value in the same way as a shop does. At this point an issue arises: the users' health token is now bound to their identity through their passport. We highlight two immediate negative consequences of this: (1) the binding can be remembered and could be used to unfairly impact users with unfavourable health token values such as when purchasing insurance or booking future flights and (2) airlines are incentivised to allow only low risk passengers on-board (to maximise flight capacity) thus reintroducing discrimination.

The problem here is caused by the *identity-binding* of the health token. While all situations are different, and thus in some *identity-binding* situations there may be possible solutions we conclude that health tokens are only suitable for *identity-free* use cases.

IV. Attacks and Analysis

In this section we first define numerous attack vectors against our system and then analyse their effect and possible mitigations.

A. Attack Vectors

All distributed systems are susceptible to Sybil attacks [4] in which an adversary impersonates another user or otherwise exploits the lack of binding between users and credentials. After Sybil attacks, we also consider adversaries who wish to learn about a user based on observing their behaviour or demanding to see their health token. We define a compromised health token to be one that is used without user consent.

a) Sybil-type A: A Sybil-type A adversary attempts to disrupt a service provider by repeatedly presenting a set of compromised tokens to a service provider. For example, if the adversary presents tokens that indicate a high level of risk, the service provider may be forced to close or act more cautiously.

b) Sybil-type B: A Sybil-type B adversary builds on the type A adversary. Here the adversary attempts to use a set of compromised tokens to attack multiple service providers. For example, an adversary could corrupt real user's phones with malware that overwrites the original certificate to the one of their choosing. The adversary's goal here could be to change government policy by artificially altering the aggregated transmission risk at a national scale.

c) Queue Observer: This adversary is interested in inferring a persons true transmission risk status by monitoring when they are allowed (and when they are refused) entry to services. We assume this adversary may be interested in monitoring a user over a long period of time.

d) Malicious Service Provider: This adversary is interested in learning a user's true transmission risk status and potentially discriminating against them based on its value. While it is likely such an adversary will be a service provider, our definition also however includes unauthorised or coercive peers.

B. Analysis of Attacks

When analysing the Sybil-type attacks we assume the adversary does not have access to a large number of valid health tokens — that is we assume they only have access to a small number of compromised certificates which they can use. On one hand this is reasonable as a valid certificate is signed by H and thus cannot be forged. On the other hand since our health tokens are not binding, a malicious user can easily use a token that was issued to someone else. Indeed, a malicious user could post their health token online for others to use should they choose. Under this informal assumption, which it is important to debate beyond this work, we show how Sybil-type attacks can be mitigated.

a) Sybil-type A: As our health tokens are non-binding, an adversary may attack a service provider by repeatedly presenting a compromised health token of their choosing. A determined adversary may even convince many users, unsuspecting or otherwise, to present a singular compromised token that has been distributed online for this purpose.

To prevent this attack a service provider can simply count the number of times each *TID* is seen in the period of a day or week. In this way a limit can be imposed on the number of times each certificate can be used over a given period of time. For an adversary to effectively use such an attack despite this mitigation they would need access to a large number of signed tokens with their desired value. In practice they would also need to convince or trick many individuals into using them.

b) Sybil-type B: By rate-limiting the number of uses of each token with respect each service provider, the adversary is limited to attempting to present each compromised token they hold the maximum number of times and to as many different service providers as possible. This adversary might try to alter the overall risk aggregates across a country, or on a smaller scale might try all the shops in a particular shopping mall or tube station.

To prevent this more widespread attack we need to monitor the usage of a certificate across multiple service providers. There are at least two methods of achieving this: (1) a central body requests and aggregates the usage count of each health token across multiple service providers and (2) the service providers communicate directly with each other to learn which certificates are being used the most — here we envisage a multi-party computation protocol might be used to do so in a privacy-preserving way.

While it is often desirable to avoid using a central authority where possible, it is likely that method (2) will both involve too large a communication overhead and place too much burden on service providers. Therefore in this work we only consider solutions using method (1). Naor et al. [15] present a secure method to find 'heavy hitting passwords' (i.e. commonly used passwords) using a central authority. This solution can also be applied here to allow a central authority to learn, in a privacy-preserving way, if there are any health tokens with an unreasonably large usage across multiple service providers. We outline the details of this approach for this application in Appendix A.

c) Queue Observer: No adversary can be confident of knowing the users true transmission risk status because the randomised response that is applied to each health token provides plausible deniability. However, an adversary who tracks a user across multiple service providers could learn (with a degree of uncertainty) a users token value.

To stop an adversary that observes multiple queues, service providers or policy makers could introduce batch admission to services. With this proviso, any information an adversary can learn by observing a user is masked by the other users in the batch.

d) Malicious Service Provider: By definition, health tokens are plausibly deniable and protect against immunity-based discrimination.

V. Limitations and Implementation

Here we discuss the limitations of our proposed approach and then demonstrate the practicality of our solution by presenting the results of our open-source implementation which can be found at [11].

A. Limitations

a) Error in aggregation: Our system perturbs a users true transmission risk with some randomness to produce a health token value. It is essential that health tokens are only used when considering a large sample of users and not for individual cases. For example, determining if a specific user is allowed into a care home is probably best left to a system with strong user-certificate binding such as [9].

We illustrate the error associated with our method by calculating the average error in computing the expected value of a health token ($E[X]$) for a set number of users. First we let $\epsilon = log\ 3$, which corresponds to outputting the correct risk status in the first step of the underlying differential privacy protocol (as described in Section II-B) with probability $\frac{1}{2}$, and show how the error changes as we increase k. Second we keep $k = 2$ constant and vary ϵ to allow for $\frac{1}{4}, \frac{1}{2}$ and $\frac{3}{4}$ chance of outputting the truth after the first (bias) coin flip in the underlying differential privacy protocol. We iterate the experiments 100 times for each number of users from 1 to 500. We see that, as expected, increasing the number of options for risk status value (increasing k) results in a larger error, as does increasing ϵ.

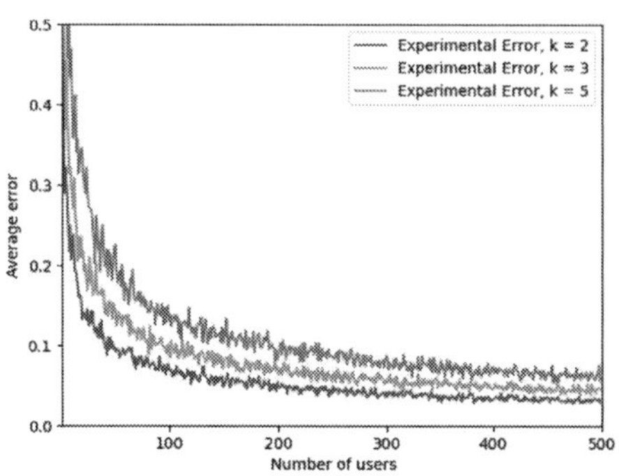

Fig. 1. The average error introduced by our system for a given number of users. We let $\epsilon = log\ (3)$ and plot the error for $k = 2, k = 3$ and $k = 5$.

b) No binding: As the tokens are not binding, their misuse is harder to mitigate or track. As the Sybil-type attacks show, it is possible that compromised certificates could be used maliciously by adversaries. It is also possible that a user will be incentivised to be tested

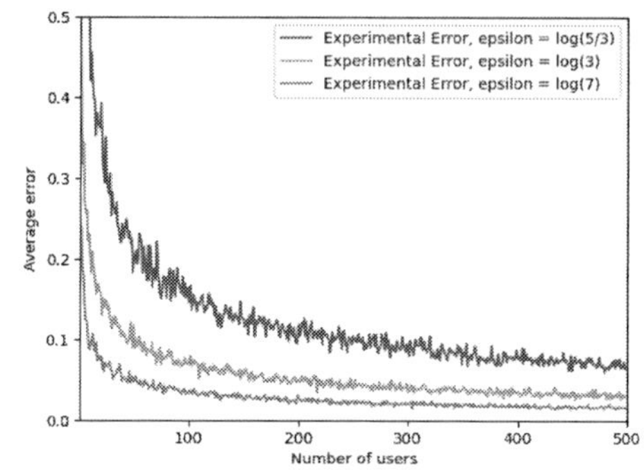

Fig. 2. The average error introduced by our system for a given number of users. We let $k = 2$ and plot the error for $\epsilon = log\ (\frac{5}{3}), \epsilon = log\ (3), \epsilon = log\ (7)$ and $k = 2$.

repeatedly until they get issued a more *desirable* health token value; In other words a user with an *undesirable* risk status may be incentivised by our system to test again (or to bribe their healthcare provider).

c) User behaviour: We cannot fully anticipate the impact of our system on user behaviour. For example, users assigned high risk values may choose not to present their health token to service providers. It may be difficult to anticipate, measure and correct for this bias.

d) National aggregation and reporting: In our system, service providers keep track of their local aggregate risk value and how many users have been in their environment during a specific period. We have not considered in this work how multiple service providers can aggregate their results and contribute to a wider geographical or national risk model. This is challenging because a service provider could be incentivised to report misinformation, particularly if restrictions on trade could be imposed as a result of reporting a high risk measurement. While it could be difficult to verify each service providers reporting, it would be possible to spot providers that continually misreport relative to their peers.

B. Implementation

We implement our system in Python using QR codes as a means of presenting and verifying a signed health token. As shown in Figure 3, our prototype allows for the generation and verification of a health token signed using 512-bit ECDSA [3].

Fig. 3. Example token generated by our prototype.

VI. Related Work and Conclusion

A. Related Work

To the best of our knowledge this is the first antibody certificate system that, by design, mitigates against immunity-based discrimination. Other proposed systems are dependant on policy and legal measures to achieve the level of non discrimination achieved by our proposal.

In [9], the secure antibody certificate system (SecureABC) was introduced that uses a standard public-key signature scheme to ensure the binding and authenticity of certificates. Likewise in [6] a system composed of W3C-standard 'verifiable credentials' [16], the 'Solid' platform for decentralised social applications [14] and a federated consortium blockchain was developed. In both these works however the user is strongly bound to their certificate. In fact it is implied that certificates are only issued to those who *pass* a test, thus not holding a certificate is synonymous with not having immunity and therefore not being immuno-privileged.

Therefore we suggest these identity-bound systems, along with similar industry led proposals [2], [10] are more applicable to situations where immunity-based discrimination can be justified. For example for workers in a care home and the identity-binding use cases we considered in Section III.

B. Conclusion

In this work we were motivated to develop a tool for measuring the viral transmission risk of groups of users which, by design, mitigates immunity-based discrimination. While there are a number of limitations to our proposed health tokens, we have shown that in identity-free situations our approach has the potential to have a net-positive benefit on society.

Acknowledgment

This work was supported by The Alan Turing Institute under the EPSRC grant EP/N510129/1

References

[1] WHO Scientific Brief - "Immunity passports" in the context of COVID-19. Online, Accessed 9 May 2020, Available at: https://www.who.int/news-room/commentaries/detail/immunity-passports-in-the-context-of-covid-19.

[2] CERTUS - A novel and simple solution for certificate issuers, holders and verifiers. Online, Accessed 19 May 2020, Available at: https://www.certusdoc.com/.

[3] Digital Signature Standard (DSS) (FIPS 186-4). Technical report, National Institute of Standards and Technology, July 2013.

[4] J. Douceur. The sybil attack. In *Proceedings of 1st International Workshop on Peer-to-Peer Systems (IPTPS)*, January 2002.

[5] M. Eisenstadt, M. Ramachandran, N. Chowdhury, A. Third, and J. Domingue. Covid-19 antibody test / vaccination certification: There's an app for that. *IEEE Open Journal of Engineering in Medicine and Biology*, pages 1–1, 2020.

[6] Marc Eisenstadt, Manoharan Ramachandran, Niaz Chowdhury, Allan Third, and John Domingue. Covid-19 antibody test / vaccination certification: There's an app for that. *IEEE Open Journal of Engineering in Medicine and Biology*, 2020.

[7] Estonia tests first digital immunity passports for workplaces. E&T editorial staff, Online, Accessed 02 June 2020, Available at: https://eandt.theiet.org/content/articles/2020/05/estonia-tests-first-digital-immunity-passports-for-workplaces/, May 2020.

[8] P. Fine, K. Eames, and D. L. Heymann. "Herd Immunity": A Rough Guide. *Clinical Infectious Diseases*, April 2011.

[9] Chris Hicks, David Butler, Carsten Maple, and Jon Crowcroft. SecureABC: Secure antibody certificates for COVID-19. *CoRR*, abs/2005.11833, 2020, (Currently under review).

[10] ImmuPass - A simple and secure certificate of COVID-19 immunity. Available at: https://www.immupass.org.

[11] Implementation available at: https://github.com/alan-turing-institute/DPHT.

[12] Ada Lovelace Institute. Rapid evidence review: Exit through the App Store. Online, Accessed 20 May 2020, Available at: https://www.adalovelaceinstitute.org/wp-content/uploads/2020/04/Ada-Lovelace-Institute-Rapid-Evidence-Review-Exit-through-the-App-Store-April-2020-2.pdf.

[13] N. Kofler and F. Baylis. Ten reasons why immunity passports are a bad idea. *Nature*, 581(7809):379–381, May 2020.

[14] E. Mansour, A. V. Sambra, S. Hawke, M. Zereba, S. Capadisli, A. Ghanem, A. Aboulnaga, and T. Berners-Lee. A demonstration of the solid platform for social web applications. In *WWW (Companion Volume)*, pages 223–226. ACM, 2016.

[15] M. Naor, B. Pinkas, and E. Ronen. How to (not) share a password: Privacy preserving protocols for finding heavy hitters with adversarial behavior. In *ACM Conference on Computer and Communications Security*, pages 1369–1386. ACM, 2019.

[16] M Sporny, D Longley, and D Chadwick. Verifiable credentials data model 1.0. *W3C Candidate Recommendation, March*, 2019.

[17] S. L. Warner. Randomized response: A survey technique for eliminating evasive answer bias. *Journal of the American Statistical Association*, 60(309):63–69, 1965. PMID: 12261830.

Appendix

Naor et al. [15] present a solution to the problem of identifying commonly used passwords – we propose their method for out situation. Similarly to identifying password outliers with respect to their frequency of use, we require a method to identify health tokens that are used so frequently that adversarial behaviour is indicated. Here we present the original solution of Naor et al. for completeness. A central authority can securely aggregate the count of health token TIDs as follows:

1) For each health token, V hashes the TID, $v_j = H(TID_j)$ — assume this is an l-bit string, in practice we suggest $l = 32$.
2) The server sends V a uniformly distributed l-bit string r_j.
3) V sends back the one bit value of the inner product of v_j and r_j over GF[2], denoted as $\langle v_j, r_j \rangle$.
4) The server keeps a table T[x] of 2^l counters, corresponding to all possible l-bit values x (initialized to zero on system setup).
5) For every value of x if $\langle x, r_j \rangle = \langle v_j, r_j \rangle$ the corresponding counter is incremented by one, otherwise it is decreased by one. Equality holds for exactly half of the values.

Let the total number of service providers that ran the protocol be N and p be the frequency of the hash value x. The expected numbers of increments and decrements are $N(p+\frac{(1-p)}{2})$ and $N\frac{(1-p)}{2}$ respectively. The expected value of the counter is $E(T[x]) = pN$. For a threshold frequency τ, the server publishes all x values such as $T[x] > \tau N$. Each V checks if $H(TID)$ is in the published hash values list. V can then act accordingly, either by discarding the certificate in the aggregation, or refusing entry to the user.

While this method can be used to detect Sybil-type B attacks there are a number of limitations to be considered. We consider three here: (1) To be practical we must efficiently increment and decrement all the counters with each certificate use, the naive approach to this requires a significant amount of memory and computational power. (2) A certificate hash will only be suspicious if, for n the total number of times any certificate is used, that one hash is used $\Omega(\sqrt{n})$ times. This could allow an attacker to use each of many certificates slightly fewer than $\sqrt{n}$ times without (most of their certificates) being detected. (3) An adversarial service provider could submit false reports of certificates with the intention of causing false alarms, this could result in legitimate users having their certificates invalidated due to a hash collision with one of those certificates.

Ovid: Message-based Automatic Contact Tracing

Leonie Reichert*, Samuel Brack*, Björn Scheuermann*†
*Humboldt University of Berlin, Department of Computer Science
{leonie.reichert, samuel.brack, scheuermann}@informatik.hu-berlin.de
†Alexander von Humboldt Institute for Internet and Society, Berlin

***Abstract*—The COVID-19 pandemic created various new challenges for our societies. Quickly discovering new infections using automated contact tracing without endangering privacy of the general public is one of these. Most discussions concerning architectures for contact tracing applications revolved around centralized against decentralized approaches. In contrast, the system proposed in this work builds on the idea of message-based contact tracing to inform users about their risk. Our main contribution is the combination of a blind-signature approach to verify infections with an anonymous postbox service. In our evaluation, we analyze all components in our system for performance and privacy, as well as security. We also derive parameters for operating our system in a pandemic scenario.**

Keywords*—COVID-19, *Contact Tracing, Privacy-Enhancing Technologies, Blind Signatures

I. Introduction

The COVID-19 pandemic challenges both emergency capacities of hospitals as well as countries democratic foundations. Contact tracing is a promising tool to combat this ongoing crisis until vaccines are ready or herd immunity is reached [1]. It allows health authorities (HA) to discover new infections by examining people that have been in contact with patients. But manual contact tracing is too slow to combat COVID-19 as it is an airborne disease and people are already infectious days before the first symptoms appear [1]. Therefore, various attempts have been made to automate the process. Some of these require the collection of large amounts of data [2]. For this reason, many activists fear that these systems could be repurposed later and turned into tools for mass surveillance [2], [3]. To address these concerns while fighting the pandemic with modern means, we propose Ovid, an automatic contact tracing (ACT) system. It uses messages to communicate risk and leaks as little information as possible to the HA. Infected users place encrypted messages in postboxes of users they have come in contact with. To provide privacy for the receiver, postboxes are combined into postbox channels and cover traffic is introduced. Message authenticity is ensured through the use of blind signatures. To the knowledge of the authors, Ovid is the first system that combines blind signatures and postbox channels with cover traffic to ensure user privacy against the HA at all times. The parameters upon which we base our evaluation provide a balance between privacy and performance. Ovid extends our work CAUDHT [4] by addressing new attack vectors and necessary architectural changes.

Our main contributions are:

- Applying blind signatures to verify the authenticity of an infection message while ensuring that the HA does not learn which users interacted.
- A defense mechanism against flooding the system with malicious messages.
- A scalable concept for cover traffic.
- An evaluation of our system.

The remainder of this paper is structured as follows. In Section II, we introduce related work concerning ACT. We explain our attacker model in Section III and our system design in Section IV. In Section V, the proposed system is evaluated. We then conclude by presenting ideas for future work on this topic.

II. Related Work

Contact tracing is the process of identifying potentially infected people by analyzing a patient's history of social contacts. This has been done for epidemics such as HIV [5] or Ebola [6]. Stochastic analysis and real world experience have proven its usefulness [5], [6]. For contact tracing to be effective, the number of identified cases has to grow faster than the number of new infections [5]. Due to increasing amounts of new patients and a high transmission rate, to stop the spreading of COVID-19 this process needs to be automated [1].

Bluetooth Low Energy (BLE) is a short-range and energy-efficient variant of Bluetooth. It supports different transmission power levels which makes it a good choice for fine-grained sensing [7]. Researchers have therefore used it for various projects revolving around interaction detection [8]. During the course of the pandemic, BLE emerged to be the most promising technology for ACT as it is available in most modern smartphones [9]. Most ACT approaches rely on users exchanging *ephemeral pseudonyms* (EPs) over BLE with others close by to register encounters and record them on their device. One drawback of using BLE for distance measurements is that calibrating devices can be challenging [10]. The smartphone app *TraceTogether* [10], released by the government of Singapore, has been the first officially running ACT system. Here, risk assessment for users is done by a central server. The server knows which users advertised which specific EP at a certain time. Infected users upload observed EPs. The server can link these to users and can thereby derive who interacted with one-another and who might be at risk. In contrast,

Workshop on Secure IT Technologies against COVID-19 (CoronaDef) 2021
21 February 2021, Virtual

https://dx.doi.org/10.14722/coronadef.2021.23010
www.ndss-symposium.org

DP-3T [11] attempts to solve the problem in a decentralized manner. In this ACT system, infected users upload their own EPs to a blackboard. Other users can check there to see if they encountered one of the published EPs. This means risk assessment is done locally on users' end devices. The blackboard server does not know who used which EPs at what time and does therefore not learn who interacted with one-another.

More closely related to the approach discussed in this paper are the ideas of Cho et al. [12]. They proposed to use private messaging to warn users who are at risk. Infected users send a warning message to mailboxes of all users they encountered. The mailbox address corresponds to the recorded advertised EP. Mailboxes are located on a central server and are reachable through proxy servers. Users regularly query all mailboxes corresponding to their past EPs for new messages. Messages have to be sent even if the user is not infected to provide cover traffic. The authors do not discuss or evaluate scalability issues of their idea. The authors also do not secure against malicious users sending false warning messages to others. In contrast to the ideas of Cho et al. Ovid's concept of cover traffic requires less overhead. Ovid also has a mechanism to defend against malicious users by employing blind signatures.

TraceSecure proposed by Bell et al. [13] builds on the ideas of Cho et al. mentioned above. Their protocol relies on multiple non-colluding parties: the HA, the government and for some cases a messaging service. When joining the system, users need to register with the government to receive a static pseudonym. An infected user warns others that are at risk by providing their history of encounters to the government. Each collected EP is encrypted individually with the government's private key. All messages created this way are then uploaded to a server belonging to the HA. The HA only accepts messages from individuals who tested positive. It passes them on to a separate government server, thereby hiding the infected user's identity. After decrypting the messages, the government knows which static pseudonyms need to be warned. It places notifications in the messaging service so that the respective users can retrieve them using their static pseudonym. This system requires cover traffic on the path from the government to the user. A related approach using direct messaging is ConTra Corona [14]. Similarly to our system, EPs advertised by users are the public part of an asymmetric key pair. The private key is uploaded to a central server. An infected individual uploads their recorded EPs to the central server using their local medical facility as relay to hide their identity. The server looks up the secret keys corresponding to uploaded private keys and marks them as infected. The server can either publish infected secret keys regularly as a list or allow users to poll. Unlike TraceSecure and ConTra Corona, Ovid does not require multiple non-colluding parties. Instead, blind signatures are used to combine the roles of the HA/medical personnel and the government. Our system also uses end-to-end cover traffic so that the entity responsible for message relay does not learn if a message recipient is at risk.

Another ACT approach is Pronto-C2 [15]. Here, users non-interactively derive a shared key from the EP they advertised during an encounter and the one they recorded. This key can only be obtained and identified by someone knowing both EPs. Infected users upload their shared keys from past encounters to a server which publishes them to all users. Users who see one of their shared keys in the published data will know that they are at risk. This approach requires that the devices of both users see each other to derive meaningful keys. It also allows an observer recording both advertised EPs to recreate the key and later on find out if one of the parties has been infected. A major difference between Pronto-C2 and Ovid is that the former leaks the EP of the infected person while the latter only reveals the corresponding time period. Also, through the use of postbox channels, users of Ovid do not need to check against all messages that have been uploaded but only against a fraction. Pronto-C2 requires additional servers to support clients during their EP exchange, while Ovid transmits all information necessary over BLE. More ACT approaches are discussed in [8].

III. Attacker Model

To understand the security requirements, we discuss several threats for ACT systems.

Malicious User: Malicious users of an ACT system can pursue several targets. They have the capability to interact with the protocol using their own client software and are not bound to use the application provided by the system or follow the protocol. One target can be the generation of false alarms to convince other users that they are at risk. Another objective of a malicious user can be attacking the availability of the system and thereby blocking the distribution of information about new infections, i. e., a denial of service (DoS). A malicious user can also be interested in deanonymizing *infected users*, meaning users that are verified COVID-19 cases.

Curious Stalker: We call a sophisticated attacker trying to stalk a specific person a curious stalker. The objective of such an attacker is to find out if the target is infected or not. The stalker can follow their victim around, at least during times when they are in a public spaces, and observe the victim's reaction and habitual changes.

Eavesdropper: An eavesdropper will try to identify users participating in the system. Its capabilities are the observation of network traffic and/or the collection of BLE beacons. Eavesdroppers can be network providers or entities with an infrastructure of Bluetooth scanners, such as billboard companies. Additionally, by observing metadata like message sizes or frequencies, this attacker can try to derive infection statuses of users.

Health Authority (HA): The HA is a government branch responsible for dealing with the COVID-19 pandemic. It manages local efforts by gathering data to contain outbreaks and conducting tests to verify cases. Thus, the HA is interested in identifying and quarantining infected patients. An overambitious HA can try to deanonymize people at risk. As a government entity the HA might also have an interest in creating a database not only containing epidemiologically relevant data but all information about users they can gather. Such a database could later be used by other governmental bodies such as law enforcement.

IV. System Design

Our system is designed to protect user privacy in during all steps of the ACT process. To this end, we propose to limit the HA's responsibility to confirming results of positively tested individuals and hosting postboxes. Thus, the amount of information the HA can derive from the protocol is minimized. Users of our system Ovid need to have the corresponding application installed on their local end devices and BLE activated to participate. These devices continuously advertise EPs over BLE so other users can record them. Each EP is a public key belonging to an asymmetric key pair. EPs are freshly generated every *epoch*, i. e., every 20 minutes, and are stored for 14 days. The locally stored *EP history* contains all EP advertised by the user during the last 14 days and the corresponding decryption keys. Recorded EPs of others are saved in the *encounter history* on the end device. When a user is confirmed as infected, they create an encrypted message for each entry in their encounter history. To prove their infection status, the user retrieves a blind signature for each message from the HA. Messages are placed in the corresponding postbox channel using the EP they are addressed to as key. A recipient will receive the message by downloading the content of the postbox channels corresponding to their past EPs. If a message is successfully decrypted and the signature is valid, the recipient knows they have been in contact with a infected user and are *at risk* of being infected.

A. Anonymous Postbox Service

Building on the ideas of Cho et al. [12], our system requires infected users to send a message for each EP in their encounter history to the corresponding *postbox*. Users periodically check all postboxes relevant to them, i. e., all postboxes corresponding to an EP they advertised during the previous 14 days. Messages in the postbox are encrypted for the user. Therefore neither the server, nor any adversary on the network can read its content. For additional protection, the postbox service needs to be designed in a way so an eavesdropper is not able to deduce a users infection status simply by checking if any messages are addressed to them. It is also important that the mere fact of accessing a specific postbox does not leak one of the user's EPs. To combat these issues, we aggregate multiple postboxes into a *postbox channel*. Messages double as cover traffic for other postboxes. Compared to ACT systems using a blackboard where every user has to download all available data, this approach requires less communication. Postbox channels consist of postboxes sharing the same prefix p, e. g., the first 20 bits of the EP. In our system channels are hosted on a single server, but they can also be distributed between several hosts.

B. Blind Signatures

Every user can download messages from all postboxes. But writing messages to postboxes needs to be handled differently. Without a verification mechanism, a malicious user can make others believe they are at risk even though no real encounter with an infected person has occurred. Another problem about not having access control is that an attacker can flood the system with invalid messages, stopping genuine messages from being delivered. Therefore, Ovid requires a signature from the HA for messages that are to uploaded to the postbox service. This ensures only users with a verified infection can place messages in postboxes. It is important that the HA does not learn the encounter history or which EPs a user used in the past when confirming someone's infection. Hence, we use *blind signatures* [16] as a mechanism for the HA to publicly verify a users infection status. To retrieve a blind signature, a user first blinds their message m which gives them the blinded message $b(m)$. For blinding, the HA's public RSA key is needed. The user then sends $b(m)$ to the HA, who signs it and returns the result $sig_{HA}(b(m))$. Unblinding this response gives the user a valid signature $sig_{HA}(m)$ over the message. The HA has not learned the contents of message m or signature $sig_{HA}(m)$.

C. Token for Retrieving a Blind Signature

Before signing a blinded message $b(m)$, the HA needs to verify the request originates from a user with a confirmed infection. People with symptoms of COVID-19 visit health care providers to get tested. When a test returns positive, *permission tokens* are passed from the health care provider to the now verified infected person. The tokens allow the infected user to retrieve blind signatures from the HA for the data they intend to upload. Each token authorizes one blind signature.

There are two ways in which these tokens can be designed. For example, the HA could centrally generate random numbers to be used as tokens and distribute them to health care providers who conduct testing. Assuming the HA is not compromised and the space from which tokes are drawn is big enough, it is not feasible for an attacker to generate fake tokens. A downside of this approach is the possible linkability of a token to a specific location or health care provider when a patient uses it to request a blind signature.

A second option is that health care providers generate and sign tokens themselves using a public key infrastructure (PKI) to distribute their public keys. This way, the HA can ensure a token originated from a valid source. To stop the HA from finding out which health care provider a user visited, a ring signature scheme [17] is used. With ring signatures, it can be verified that one of a predefined set of keys was used for signing, but not which specific one. This means the actual signer (here a health care provider) is not linkable to the signature. The ring signature's size grows linearly with the number of signers in the ring [18]. It would become impractical to have one ring of all health care providers, both in terms of signature verification complexity and size of the ring's public key. We propose to form smaller rings consisting of several health care providers each to ensure a balance between signature size and anonymity set. This keeps key sizes manageable and allows for member changes in the system without having to discard the entire signature ring. To prevent a curious HA from estimating the geo-location of an infected patient presenting a token, each ring is filled randomly so that all ring members are distributed over the HA's territory.

Ovid uses this mechanism for token generation. Here, tokens consist of a unique 256 bit random number and a timestamp, as well as a signature. The timestamp has a granularity of 14 days and is used prevent an attacker from replaying recorded tokens to generate additional blind signatures. A signature over random number and timestamp verifies the authenticity of the token to the HA. The token is generated and signed by the health care provider who hands it out using a ring signature scheme. After a token was used by the infected user, it is placed on a blacklist maintained by the HA. Blacklisted entries can be discarded after 14 days have passed because of the timestamp in the tokens.

D. Infection Messages

An newly-diagnosed infected user needs to spread the news quickly to all users they came across while being contagious (maximum the last 14 days). Assume Alice encountered Bob and recorded Bob's EP pk_{Bob} (which is also a public key). Several days later she tests positive for COVID-19. To warn Bob, Alice creates an infection message. She first encrypts the epoch of the encounter t_e with pk_{Bob} and appends the current time t_m. Alice then blinds this string to retrieve a blind signature from the HA. The permission token required to retrieve a signature was given to Alice by the health care provider she visited to get tested for COVID-19. Alice appends the signature to the first part, constructing the infection message m. The format for m is as follows:

$$m = E_{pk_{Bob}}(t_e)||t_m||sig_{sk_{HA}}(E_{pk_{Bob}}(t_e)||t_m) \quad (1)$$

Alice stores m in the postbox channel corresponding to pk_{Bob}, which is given by $truncate(pk_{Bob}, p)$ (see Figure 1). The function $truncate(x, p)$ returns the first p bits of x. Alice will warn all other users she encountered during the relevant time period using this pattern. Having t_m as part of the infection message gives the postbox server the ability to figure out how old a signature is. The postbox server does not accept infection messages with a timestamp t_m in the future and can remove those older than the maximum incubation time. Since the signature covers t_m, an attacker can not overload the postbox system by replaying old infection messages.

To hinder an eavesdropper located on the network from figuring out if Bob received an infection message, cover traffic is required. Aggregating postboxes into postbox channels gives Bob plausible deniability, but this might not be enough if there are only few messages in the system. Therefore, when Alice receives her bulk of permission tokens from her health care provider which allows her to retrieve signatures, she might receive more than she asked for. The probability for additional tokens can be either fixed or dependent on the current utilization of the system. After obtaining signatures for all entries in her history of encounters, Alice creates random messages and fetches valid signatures for these by using her remaining permission tokens. These cover messages are addressed to random postboxes. When Alice places all her messages in the postbox system, the server will not be able to differentiate between real infection messages and signed cover traffic. This means only infected users can create cover traffic.

E. Postbox Retrieval Mechanism

Users need to query their postboxes periodically if they want to determine whether they are at risk.

Assume Bob met Alice recently and used the EP pk_{Bob} at that time. Alice has now been diagnosed and left a message in Bob's postbox at the channel associated with pk_{Bob}. If Bob performs a search for the truncated EP in the postbox service all messages from this postbox channel will be returned. He will attempt to decrypt all returned messages using the private key corresponding to pk_{Bob} and succeed with Alice message. To give Bob a fast way to check if the decryption of $E_{pk_{Bob}}(t_e)$

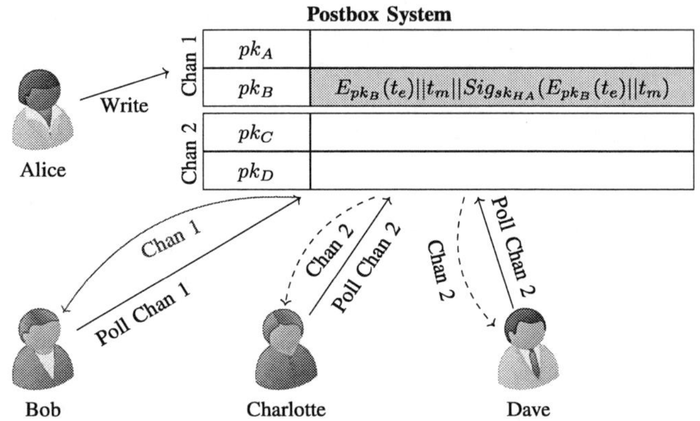

Fig. 1. An example how messages are uploaded and retrieved for a postbox service with two postboxes per channel. Alice places an infection message for Bob who retrieves it by fetching the contents of the channel corresponding to pk_b from the postbox system.

was successful, a fixed amount of zeros can be added to the beginning of t_e before it is encrypted. This way Bob knows the message was addressed to him. The signature part of the message confirms to him that Alice's test result were indeed positive. The decryption gives Bob the timestamp t_e of their encounter. He performs a sanity check to verify that pk_{Bob} was actually advertised during that time. This stops an attacker who tries to create false warning by collecting EPs in a low-risk area and replaying them later in a high-risk area. Since no part of the message contains any information relating to Alice, Bob will not learn that the message was created by her. It is possibly to include e.g. Alice's EP at t_e in the infection message. This allows Bob to learn which EP belongs to a person that send him an infection warning. Using the logs, it would make it easier for him to deanonymize Alice.

Users are notified by their end device that they are at risk after a certain threshold of exposure to infected users is exceeded. This threshold needs to be defined by epidemiologists. Since risk assessment is done locally, it is possible to take individual risk factors into account without endangering user privacy. Such factors can be the their medical history or the general infection risk in their area.

F. Operation

To ensure that the system is operated in a secure and privacy-preserving manner, it is important to consider some implementation details. A theoretically secure system can be dangerous for users if the operator uses outdated cryptographic functions or if the end-user app is contains security vulnerabilities.

Our first consideration is the correct key management and distribution. For the blind signatures to be verifiable and secure against manipulations from a network operator, a secure channel for the HA's public key to the end user is required. The end user app needs to be able to verify the HA's key, which is why the HA needs their key either signed by a widespread SSL certificate provider or directly embedded into the end user app. Theoretically, the connection to the HA doesn't need to be secured itself because the blind signature scheme itself provides a verification mechanism for the receiver of the signature. To prevent a denial of service by the network operator who could block packets with messages containing blind signature requests it can still be beneficial to use an SSL secured connection. To verify tokens, the HA needs the public key for all rings of health care providers. This can be either done via direct communication or also using a PKI. On the client side it is important to have a proper key store for managing the secret keys in the app. These keys should be stored in encrypted storage sections if the operating system offers such a service. Alternatively, the app could prompt the user with a password request to encrypt their secret keys. Such a prompt has to be carefully designed however so that usability (and thus usage) is not harmed by a complex user interface.

In case of a high infection risk, users should be notified fast. This requires users to poll the postbox services in short intervals. To support this traffic overhead, a scalable infrastructure is required to handle the load, such as a content delivery network. When sending a request to retrieve a postbox channel, users can send the time stamp of their last request. The server can then return only messages that the user has not received so far. This deceases the network load for users and for the postbox service. Users have to decrypt all messages they receive to find out if they are at risk. Decryption of messages in asymmetric encryption schemes is an CPU intensive task and therefore requires more energy. For this reason, this task should be executed when the user's end device is charging or the battery is reasonably full. But at least once per day, all new messages need to be decrypted to ensure timely notification.

V. Evaluation

We evaluated our system with a set of performance experiments and analyzed its security and privacy.

A. Security and Privacy Analysis

There is a wide range of possible attacks against ACT systems. We discuss them with the focus on Ovid.

1) Malicious Users: A malicious or non-compliant infected user can always decide to not upload data to the HA. This is due to the voluntary nature of this system. Forcing people to install contact tracing applications and demanding user to upload their data is not an option in many western countries as it would undermine the rights of citizens without (compatible) end devices [19]. We therefore consider participation as voluntary.

Malicious users can check the epoch t_e for which they received an infection message. Using their memory to remember who they encountered during this time, they can *deanonymize infected users*. Malicious users can not deanonymize infected individuals they did not encounter. To achieve a higher accuracy during deanonymization, a *one-contact attack* can be performed. Here, for each encounter a new profile is generated. This binds each of the attacker's EPs uniquely to a encounter, as well as a (self-recorded) location and time. However, this attack can not be launched retroactively.

In a *replay attack*, the attacker captures BLE beacons from a low-risk location, such as a supermarket, and replays them in a high-risk environment, such as a hospital, to target a specific person or clientele. To limit the impact of such an attack the epoch of the encounter is part of the infection message in Ovid. The only option for the attacker is therefore to *relay* EPs during the same epoch. Proposals to use an active protocol to stop this attack such as [20] are problematic, as this opens new ways to exploit Bluetooth end devices. In [21], the author proposes to broadcast parts of the GPS locations together with the EP. So by revealing some location information to others close by the attack is mitigated.

A *false notification/black market attack* has the goal to send infection messages to users who are not at risk. To do so, an attacker needs to obtain valid EPs to send messages to e. g., through recording advertisements or through black market exchanges. An attacker simply guessing EPs is not considered a threat for Ovid because the space from which EPs are drawn is too big. To execute the attack, the adversary needs a permission token to retrieve a valid signature from the HA (e. g., from an online black market). They then place an infection message in the corresponding postbox. As long as the epoch of the encounter t_e matches the epoch in which the target used the corresponding EP, the target will falsely assume that the massage is valid. To mitigate false notification attacks the message format could be extended to contain a signature over the EP of the infected user used during the encounter.

2) Curious Stalker: A curious stalker Sam can capture EPs of his target Tiffany and snoop on the corresponding postbox channels. Cover traffic stops him from being sure if there are real infection messages for Tiffany. For rates of cover traffic of at least 10% and more than two users per channel, this attack becomes inefficient (see Figure 2).

3) Health Authority: The HA plays an important role in our system. It is crucial for our privacy goals to ensure that the HA can not use its special position in the system to endanger user privacy. An obvious way for the HA to gain additional knowledge is to *analyze metadata*. An infection message can be matched to an infected user Alice by storing the IP address from where it was uploaded. To mitigate this, Alice needs to use a Tor-like [22] anonymisation network which hides her IP address through multiple indirections. She has to use a new circuit for every infection message to ensure unlinkability. An anonymisation service is also useful when infected users try to retrieve signatures from the HA. When checking postboxes it is not necessary to use this form of anonymisation because of the cover traffic. The HA can also conduct a *timing attack*, as sender will upload messages as soon as they are created. As mitigation, an infected Alice can spread out her uploads over several hours. As this delays the time at which users at risk receive a risk notification the uploads should not be spread out too far.

4) Eavesdroppers: An eavesdropper who listens for BLE traffic can try to *re-identify* and *track users*. For this purpose we set the epoch length to 20 min. A longer period increases the possibility of location tracking [8], a shorter period requires more channels and decryption overhead in Ovid.

An eavesdropper only listing to network traffic can not derive if messages received by a user are infection messages that contain a warning. This is because real messages for a specific user are hidden between real messages for other users and cover traffic. The use of a Tor-like network also hinders this eavesdropper from finding out who is infected, as it becomes difficult to *recognize who sends infection messages*

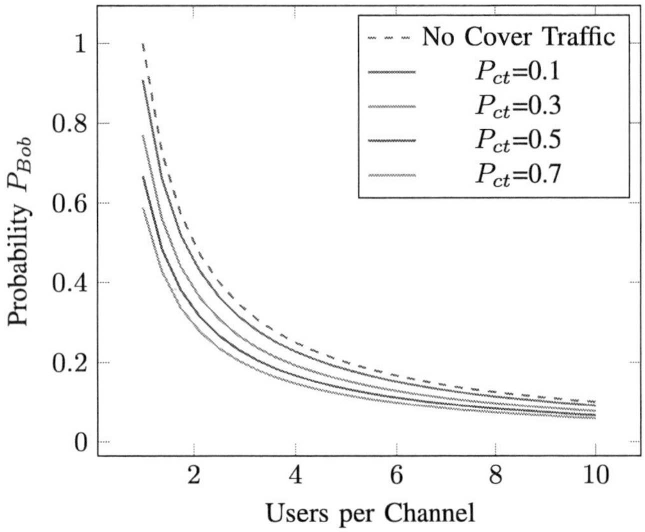

Fig. 2. This graph shows the probability if a message in a channel is designated for user Bob who accesses the channel. It is plotted against the number of users m per channel. Each curve illustrates a different probability P_{ct} representing the likelihood with which a user uploads an additional cover message for each real message. For this purpose the probability of how likely it is for a packet to be addressed to Bob $\frac{1}{m}$ is combined with the probability that a packet is not considered as cover traffic $1 - \frac{P_{ct}}{1+P_{ct}}$. This gives us: $P_{Bob} = \frac{1}{m} \cdot (1 - \frac{P_{ct}}{1+P_{ct}})$.

to the HA's server. This does not completely stop this attacker as timing attacks are a general problem of Tor [23]. Instead, mix-nets as described in [24] could be used as anonymisation service, because they are designed to protect against timing attacks.

A more powerful version of the deanonymization attack presented in Section V-A1 can be conducted by an eavesdropper with access to widely deployed BLE scanners, such as billboard companies or hackers gaining access to their infrastructure. If the network of scanners is tightly knit, the attacker can use recorded data to derive a users location history by linking consecutive EPs. By equipping scanners with cameras this attacker can deanonymize people that become infected at a later point in time. All Bluetooth/BLE-based systems known to the authors are exposed to such attacks [8], [25].

B. Performance

To assess the practical feasibility of our approach, we conducted a performance evaluation using a Python REST server. It provides blind signatures, stores infection messages uploaded by infected users and distributes them to requesting users. The server runs on a machine with three dedicated Intel® Xeon® E5-2643v2 cores and 8 GB of RAM. The client is capable of creating infection messages and querying the server for messages using its past EPs.

First, we evaluate the performance needed by the HA server. The server is capable of providing 4651.16 ± 259.55 blind signatures per second (10 runs on localhost). Here and in the following, error intervals represent the standard deviation. Generating blind signatures can be parallelized by sharing the HA secret key with several physical machines. Even in scenarios where a single infected user uploads hundreds of messages the system remains scalable.

Our second focus lies on the performance of the backend database. To be able to easily discard entries that are older than 14 days, the time-series database influxdb was used. Storing 10,000 messages in influxdb took $6.33 \pm 0.73s$ (10 runs on localhost).

In our third experiment we asses the system's reporting performance over an 100 MBit fiber Internet connection in a large setup, with a delay of 50 ms. We simulate 3,000 clients on an Intel® Core® i7-8550U and 16 GB of RAM. Clients use encounter histories generated by a script. Each user is assigned a number. Encounters are created by drawing two numbers from a uniform distribution where each number represents a user. The corresponding epoch is derived similarly by drawing a discrete time interval from a uniform distribution. For each encounter the corresponding history files are updated by appending the other side's public key from that epoch. Each history contains 100 encounters on average. During the simulation, clients create and upload infection messages for all of their generated encounters. With a probability of P_{ct} the client receives an additional permission token per requested token. These additional tokens are the used to create random messages for cover traffic. P_{ct} is set to 0.1 as Figure 2 shows that higher levels of cover traffic do not come with additional privacy. We do not consider a probability of less than 0.1 for cover traffic, as the parameter ensures that some artificial messages are stored on the server. This is especially relevant in situations with low infection rates and thus few real messages. The average reporting time is $279.33 \pm 142.27s$ for a client over the previously described Internet connection. Users who do not create infection messages were not simulated as they only query the server but otherwise do not impact the system.

In our final experiment we evaluate the retrieval and decryption performance of a client. Again, we simulate 3,000 clients as described in the previous experiment. We assume that a channel is identified by the first 19 bit of the recipient's public key, resulting in 2^{19} channels. This provides a relatively large anonymity set even in scenarios where infection rates are low and leads to a little more than 5 users per channel on average. As can be seen in Figure 2, such an anonymity level seems reasonable to us, as more users per channel only slightly improves anonymity, but increases load on the network and decryption times on the client. Users have 1008 EPs, which corresponds to a new EP every 20 min over the course of two weeks. This means a user has to query approximately 1008 postbox channels. The level of cover traffic P_{ct} is set to 0.1. A client retrieves all channels that correspond to its EPs and attempts to decrypt the messages contained in them. If a message is decrypted successfully, the risk score is updated. The average duration to retrieve and decrypt infection messages from postboxes covering the last 14 days was $79.80 \pm 27.83s$ (100 runs over the Internet). Although decrypting messages for a user is a resource-intensive task, performing it once a day appears to be feasible on mobile devices.

VI. Conclusion and Future Work

In this paper, we presented Ovid, a new approach for automated contact tracing using Bluetooth Low Energy. We combine blind signatures for anonymous infection verification with the idea of anonymous postboxes to warn users that they might be infectious. We ensure that the central health authority does not learn the identity of infected individuals or of people they encountered. Additionally, our system protects against several attacker types. Most notably, malicious users trying to cause panic by creating false warnings and curious parties interested in learning the risk status of a target are stopped.

In our evaluation, we show parameters for which the system can be operated in a real-world scenario. The biggest performance bottleneck consists of the decryption step on the user's mobile device. Decrypting large amounts of asymmetrically encrypted data requires notable computation time. This results in natural limitations for channel sizes, which also helps to keep networking requirements lower. The steps performed on the central server are scalable and can be distributed in case a single machine becomes unable to serve incoming requests.

We envision our future work in improving client performance and in exploring alternatives to the postbox service. An idea to relieve weak client systems would be to outsource decryption to a more powerful device that is also under the user's control, e. g., their laptop or a server they trust. It should however always be guaranteed that private keys remain under the control of the user who generated them.

ACKNOWLEDGMENT

The authors would like to thank Martin Florian, Manuel Herrmann and Marcel Pazelt for their helpful input.

REFERENCES

[1] L. Ferretti *et al.*, "Quantifying SARS-CoV-2 transmission suggests epidemic control with digital contact tracing," *Science*, vol. 368, no. 6491, 2020.

[2] M. Burgess, "Coronavirus contact tracing apps were meant to save us. They won't," www.wired.co.uk/article/contact-tracing-apps-coronavirus, 2020, accessed: 02. December 2020.

[3] J. Larus *et al.*, "Joint statement on contact tracing: Date 19th april 2020," www.esat.kuleuven.be/cosic/sites/contact-tracing-joint-statement/, 2020, accessed: 02. December 2020.

[4] S. Brack, L. Reichert, and B. Scheuermann, "Decentralized contact tracing using a dht and blind signatures," Cryptology ePrint Archive, Report 2020/398, 2020.

[5] K. T. Eames and M. J. Keeling, "Contact tracing and disease control," *P ROY SOC B-BIOL SCI*, vol. 270, no. 1533, pp. 2565–2571, 2003.

[6] G. Webb, C. Browne, X. Huo, O. Seydi, M. Seydi, and P. Magal, "A model of the 2014 Ebola epidemic in West Africa with contact tracing," *PLoS currents*, vol. 7, 2015.

[7] S. Bertuletti, A. Cereatti, U. D. Croce, M. Caldara, and M. Galizzi, "Indoor distance estimated from bluetooth low energy signal strength: Comparison of regression models," in *IEEE Sensors Applications Symposium*. Catania, Italy: IEEE, 2016, pp. 1–5. [Online]. Available: doi.org/10.1109/SAS.2016.7479899

[8] L. Reichert, S. Brack, and B. Scheuermann, "A survey of automatic contact tracing approaches," Cryptology ePrint Archive, Report 2020/672, 2020.

[9] Bluetooth SIG, Inc., "2020 bluetooth market update," 2020, accessed: 02. December 2020. [Online]. Available: www.bluetooth.com/bluetooth-resources/2020-bmu/

[10] Government of Singapore, "TraceTogether," 2020, accessed: 02. December 2020. [Online]. Available: www.tracetogether.gov.sg

[11] C. Troncoso *et al.*, "Decentralized Privacy-Preserving Proximity Tracing," 2020, accessed: 02. December 2020. [Online]. Available: www.github.com/DP-3T/documents

[12] H. Cho, D. Ippolito, and Y. W. Yu, "Contact tracing mobile apps for COVID-19: privacy considerations and related trade-offs," *CoRR*, vol. abs/2003.11511, 2020.

[13] J. Bell, D. Butler, C. Hicks, and J. Crowcroft, "Tracesecure: Towards privacy preserving contact tracing," *CoRR*, vol. abs/2004.04059, 2020. [Online]. Available: arxiv.org/abs/2004.04059

[14] W. Beskorovajnov, F. Dörre, G. Hartung, A. Koch, J. Müller-Quade, and T. Strufe, "ConTra Corona: Contact tracing against the coronavirus by bridging the centralized–decentralized divide for stronger privacy," Cryptology ePrint Archive, Report 2020/505, 2020.

[15] G. Avitabile, V. Botta, V. Iovino, and I. Visconti, "Towards defeating mass surveillance and sars-cov-2: The Pronto-C2 fully decentralized automatic contact tracing system," Cryptology ePrint Archive, Report 2020/493, 2020.

[16] D. Chaum, "Blind signatures for untraceable payments," in *CRYPTO*. Plenum Press, New York, 1982, pp. 199–203.

[17] R. L. Rivest, A. Shamir, and Y. Tauman, "How to leak a secret," in *ASIACRYPT*, ser. Lecture Notes in Computer Science, vol. 2248. Springer, 2001, pp. 552–565.

[18] J. K. Liu and D. S. Wong, "On the security models of (threshold) ring signature schemes," in *International Conference on Information Security and Cryptology*. Springer, 2004, pp. 204–217.

[19] A. Jelinek, "EDPB letter concerning the european commission's draft guidance on apps supporting the fight against the covid-19 pandemic," 2020, accessed: 02. December 2020. [Online]. Available: edpb.europa.eu/our-work-tools/our-documents/letters/edpb-letter-concerning-european-commissions-draft-guidance-apps_en

[20] S. Vaudenay, "Analysis of DP3T," Cryptology ePrint Archive, Report 2020/399, 2020.

[21] K. Pietrzak, "Delayed authentication: Preventing replay and relay attacks in private contact tracing," Cryptology ePrint Archive, Report 2020/418, 2020.

[22] R. Dingledine, N. Mathewson, and P. F. Syverson, "Tor: The second-generation onion router," in *USENIX*. San Diego, CA, USA: USENIX, 2004, pp. 303–320.

[23] R. Nithyanand, O. Starov, P. Gill, A. Zair, and M. Schapira, "Measuring and mitigating as-level adversaries against tor," in *NDSS*. San Diego, CA, USA: The Internet Society, 2016.

[24] G. Danezis, R. Dingledine, and N. Mathewson, "Mixminion: Design of a type III anonymous remailer protocol," in *IEEE Security and Privacy*. Berkeley, CA, USA: IEEE Computer Society, 2003, pp. 2–15.

[25] Fraunhofer AISEC, "Pandemic contact tracing apps:DP-3T, PEPP-PT NTK, and ROBERT from a privacy perspective," Cryptology ePrint Archive, Report 2020/489, 2020.

Hashomer – Privacy-Preserving Bluetooth Based Contact Tracing Scheme for Hamagen

Benny Pinkas
Bar-Ilan University, Israel
benny@pinkas.net

Eyal Ronen
Tel Aviv University, Israel
eyal.ronen@cs.tau.ac.il

***Abstract*—In recent months multiple proposals for contact tracing schemes for combating the spread of COVID-19 have been published. Many of those proposals try to implement this functionality in a decentralized and privacy-preserving manner using Bluetooth Low Energy (BLE).**

In this paper, we present "Hashomer", our proposal for a contact tracing scheme tailored for the Israeli Ministry of Health's (MoH) "Hamagen" application. The design is fully decentralized, and has the following properties:

- Message Unlinkability — Different BLE messages sent by the same user cannot be linked to each other (except for messages sent by COVID-19 positive users who *give consent* to tracing their contacts, and only for messages sent within a *short* time period).

- Explainability — To convince users that they were exposed to a COVID-19 positive person, we let them learn the approximate time of contact. This also implies that users can potentially learn, using the phone's GPS information, the location of the exposure.

- Partial Disclosure and Coercion Prevention — Users and the MoH are able to redact tracing information and exposure notifications for specific time intervals.

- Prevention of Relay Attacks – The design prevents attacks where a malicious receiver relays BLE transmissions from one location to other locations.

- Proof of exposure to a COVID-19 positive person — To prevent false reports about exposure, we allow users who are notified by the application about an exposure to a COVID-19 positive person, to prove this fact to the server.

- Identity Commitment — To prevent malicious changing or replacing keys, we bind the BLE messages to a unique ID in a privacy-preserving way.

- Performance — BLE payload size is limited to 16 bytes. The application uses only symmetric key cryptography (AES and HMAC). To reduce bandwidth, contact updates from the MoH are of limited size. Moreover, the local search for exposure is linear in the number of messages and number of COVID-19 positive persons.

I. INTRODUCTION

We describe a design for a BLE-based contact tracing application which was consequently developed by the Israeli Ministry of Health (MoH), and deployed in July 2020 under the name Hamagen 2. A reference python implementation of our design can be found at https://github.com/eyalr0/HashomerCryptoRef.

The design is based on two main principles:

- Empowering end-users: The system is decentralized, in the sense that all information is stored locally and is controlled by the users. Only users, and not the government, are informed about exposures to COVID-19 positive persons. The decision on how to behave given this warning is made by the user.
  In order to improve "explainability", namely to convince users to have confidence in the warnings given by the system, it provides users with accurate and fine-grained information about exposures. In addition, to obtain users' trust, the system respects their privacy and enables them to control the information that is revealed if they become COVID-19 positive.
- Preventing attacks: Any attack against the system, or even a publication of the feasibility of such an attack, might reduce public trust and prevent users from using the system or adhering to its exposure notifications. The resulting effect on the public acceptance of the system might be more severe than the immediate results of the attack. We therefore took additional efforts to prevent sophisticated attacks on the trustworthiness of the system. This was done while keeping within the requirements of smooth operation on commodity phones.

The design follows the same structure as other designs for decentralized contact tracing, such as DP-3T [12], Google and Apple [1], and PACT [5]. Namely, each phone sends short BLE messages with random ephemeral ids, and stores similar messages that it receives. When a user is identified as COVID-19 positive, the user can provide the MoH with information that can be broadcasted to all users, allowing them to learn whether they received BLE messages from this user.

A. Privacy, Security and Operational Requirements

We would first like to emphasize several very basic privacy features that this design supports:

1) To guarantee privacy, all information is stored locally. **No messages are ever sent from the application to any server, except for *voluntary* messages by COVID-19 positive persons, or by users who were**

Workshop on Secure IT Technologies against COVID-19 (CoronaDef) 2021
21 February 2021, Virtual

https://dx.doi.org/10.14722/coronadef.2021.23011
www.ndss-symposium.org

notified (by the application) about an exposure to another COVID-19 positive user and wishes to report this.

2) The ephemeral IDs sent in short-range BLE messages are computed from keys which are generated in the device, and look pseudo-random to any other entity.
3) The decision whether to reveal contact tracing information is made by the user, and is completely voluntary. Similarly, a notification about exposure to a COVID-19 positive person is shown locally in the application, and is kept hidden from the MoH unless the user wishes to report it.
4) The application does not reveal to the MoH any location information, not even of COVID-19 positive persons.
5) The design *allows the user to "snooze"* sending BLE messages in privacy critical situations (e.g., a journalist meeting with a confidential source). It also *allows users to retroactively delete keys* associated with specific time intervals.
6) The design *allows users to delete their history of exposure alerts*. This feature is needed to prevent other parties, such as employers, from coercing users to prove that they have not received any exposure alerts.

The system must address the following security issues:

1) Prevention of relay attacks, in which an attacker receives messages sent by users of the application in one location, for example, an emergency room in a hospital, and transmits them in different locations (say, busy train stations). Such an attack might cause unnecessary warnings showed to users.
2) Identity commitment — A malicious attacker might try to replace or change keys. For example, a disgruntled employee might want to cause all of his coworkers to self-isolate. To accomplish that, he will bribe a COVID-19 positive person to upload the keys from his phone.
3) Prevention of "fake" exposures – The design prevents users from claiming that they were in contact with an infected person. Some users might opt to do so, for instance, if they want to get a sick leave for the required quarantine period. Note that a user who had a real contact with an infected person can always transfer this information to other users, and then these users will be able to fake a contact. However, the server can become suspicious and do more checks if too many people use the same verification information.
4) Cloning and copying attacks – A sophisticated attacker might clone multiple phones to use the same master key, or copy keys from a phone of an infected person. We do not protect against these attacks.

B. Related Work

A lot of effort has been invested in designing and implementing contact tracing applications. Decentralized contact tracing applications do not keep a central database which records users' contacts, but rather keep this information on users' devices and inform only the users, and no central authority, of contacts with COVID-19 positive persons. Currently the major application that is rolled out across Europe is DP-3T [12]. Another decentralized design, called PACT, was designed by researchers from MIT and other institutes [3]. Centralized contact tracing applications give the government information about exposures. An example of such an application is the TraceTogether application of Singapore [8]. See, for example, [6], [11], for more thorough surveys of contact tracing applications.

Mobile operating system make it hard for applications which run in the background to send and receive BLE communication, and to do this with minimal battery consumption. Apple and Google developed a special API, called GAEN, which supports BLE communication for contact tracing applications. The usage of this API is limited for government applications which agree with usage terms defined by Apple and Google [1].

Security issues with the current designs were identified, e.g. in [13], [4], and demonstrated in [2]. A design which addresses some of these issues was presented in [9] (but not accompanied by an implementation).

There are also contact tracing designs which are based on more advanced cryptographic primitives, such as zero-knowledge proofs of or group signatures, e.g. [7], [14], but these desgins are less efficient, and are not accompanied by any proof-of-concept implementations.

II. Technical Overview

The basic strawman design for a contact tracing scheme has each instance of the application send short random messages (ephemeral IDs) over BLE. The application also records all BLE messages that it receives. During normal operation, the application never sends anything over any other communication channel. The only exception is when the user is identified as COVID-19 positive (and has a code received from the MoH that verifies this fact). Then the user can *explicitly request* to provide the ministry of Health with all the ephemeral IDs that were sent by his copy of the application in the last 14 days.[1] The MoH periodically distributes these values, received from all new COVID-19 positive persons, to all users, where for each time period the MoH sends all corresponding ephemeral IDs in random order. Then any copy of the application can locally check if it previously received any of these ephemeral IDs over BLE, and use a local algorithm to alert the user to the risk of contact with the corona virus (for example, alert the user if ephemeral IDs were consecutively received in any period of 15 minutes.) The user is then able to inform the MoH that he or she were in contact with a COVID-19 positive person.

This initial design provides privacy for all receiving users since no information is sent from their phones, except for short *random* BLE messages. The BLE messages can be generated in each personal copy of the application based on a secret random seed, and look pseudo-random to all other users. The privacy of COVID-19 positive persons is preserved in the sense that it is impossible to link different BLE messages of the same person.

[1] We assume in this paper that epidemiological contact tracing needs to identify all people who were in contact with the COVID-19 positive person in the last 14 days.

This basic scheme has a scalabily issue: Suppose that users change their ephemeral IDs every 5 minutes. Then every user sends more than 4000 ephemeral IDs in the 14 day period. In this case an update message for about 1000 or 10000 new COVID-19 positive persons will be too large. (This is true irrespectively of the compression method that is used, such as a Bloom filter or a Cuckoo filter, as long as we want to keep the false positive probability low.)

Daily seeds: An appealing option is for the client to use a separate seed per day, and use it to derive all ephemeral IDs of that day. In this case the MoH needs to send only 14 seeds per COVID-19 positive person. This approach is currently used by GAEN. However, this approach suffers from some drawbacks: The privacy of the COVID-19 positive persons is affected since it is now possible to link different ephemeral IDs sent by the same person in the same day. The client application needs to generate all ephemeral IDs from the seeds, and this task might be computationally heavy. In addition, it is impossible to redact less than an entire day of the BLE message history of COVID-19 positive persons, namely have the MoH send an update broadcast which does not include some of the ephemeral IDs sent by a COVID-19 positive person. (The redaction feature is important for privacy, efficiency, and accuracy.)

A. The "Hashomer" Design

While the basic idea and design are similar to that of other designs, and in particular DP-3T [12], our design has some privacy and security features which are not present in most other contact tracing designs. We list here the main differences with respect to the DP-3T design.

1) A hybrid design: An initial master key is generated when the application is installed, and a chain of daily master keys is generated from that key. The application keeps the master day key of 14 days ago, and erase all prior keys. Each day is divided to epochs (e.g., hours), and each epoch is divided to time units (e.g., 5 minutes). Every epoch has a different epoch key which is generated from the daily key. The ephemeral ID is changed each time unit, and is derived from the current epoch key. When it is needed to report the ephemeral IDs sent by a COVID-19 positive person, only relevant epoch keys that were used by the person are broadcast to all users.

2) Message Unlinkability: Different BLE messages sent by the same user are pseudo-random and cannot be linked to each other. The goal is to prevent tracking of specific users. The only exception it users who were found to be COVID-19 positive. If such a user agrees to notify their contact, the keys required to identify their messages are uploaded to the MoH servers, and are broadcast to all users. Other applications broadcast keys which enable to link messages sent by the user over relatively long periods of time (a day). Our design has the message-linkability period (epoch) as a parameter, which is currently set to be equal to one hour.

3) Tradeoff Between Privacy and Explainability: The DP-3T design prioritizes the privacy of the positive person and therefore provides to exposed users only a coarse time window of the exposure (e.g., Tuesday morning). We believe that explainability is important in order to convince users to quarantine themselves.[2] Therefore, the application provide users with a more fine-grained time frame about the exposure. Using the device's locally stored GPS history, the application can also provide the user with an approximated location of the exposure.

4) Partial Disclosure: Our design lets the user or MoH redact all tracing information for specific periods of time. This is useful for privacy (for example, letting users redact private meetings which they want to hide), and for efficiency (e.g., redacting times when it is known that the user was alone), and for accuracy (e.g., redacting times where user was stuck in a traffic jam) . To facilitate this, we use a tree structure for key derivation, allowing the MoH to broadcast only a subset of the keys. Although the DP-3T white-paper suggests two variants that support partial disclosures, they require more bandwidth and, as far as we know, are not used in practice.

5) Prevention of Relay Attacks: A potential attack scenario is where an attacker relays messages from one location where COVID-19 positive persons are likely to appear (e.g., an emergency room) to many other busy locations, thus causing many false reports of exposure to positive persons.

To overcome this attack we incorporate the coarse-grain location data of the place of contact into the protocol. The BLE message therefore includes an encryption of coarse geo-location information (e.g., accuracy of ± 500 meters), and a MAC to verify its authenticity. The receiver stores the location in which it received this message. The encryption and authentication keys are only revealed voluntarily by confirmed infected persons. The BLE message *is never sent to the server*, but can be used by the receiver to verify that it was in close physical proximity to the infected sender.

We note that the explainability property requires the receiver to save rather fine-grained timing information, which the receiver can combine with its personal location data. This implicitly enables the receiver to identify locations of contact with COVID-19 positive persons, and therefore the fact that we incorporate encrypted location data in the protocol does not give any new capabilities to the receiver.

The relay prevention feature is optional. If either party (sender or receiver) does not have location information, relay prevention will be disabled for the specific interaction (the relevant party will send or store a NULL symbol as location). As the location information is MACed, malicious relays cannot "remove" location information. As long as a large majority of the users have location information, this mitigation will still be effective.

6) Proof of exposure to a COVID-19 positive person: In some cases, users might falsely report that they were exposed to a COVID-19 positive person, to gain benefits such as priority in COVID-19 testing or a paid sick leave. We, therefore, add an option for users to prove this exposure. This is done by defining part of the ephemeral ID as a function of a verification key. When a user is identified as COVID-19 positive, he or she sends the verification keys to the MoH, but they are not broadcast to all users.

[2]This requirement might depend on the culture and values of different countries. We believe that in many countries, and at least when the system begins rolling out, users will require an explanation for an exposure notification.

Even without these keys, users are still able to identify ephemeral IDs sent by COVID-19 positive persons. They can prove the exposure by providing the part of the ephemeral ID, which depends on the verification key. (The challenge is supporting this feature while keeping the size of the ephemeral IDs to be only 16 bytes)

We note that sending this proof discloses to the MoH's server the specific positive person to whom a user was exposed, so this ability remains optional.

7) Identity Commitment: We want to prevent adversaries from having multiple devices send the same ephemeral IDs. When installing the application, the users commit to a unique ID, that can be an official government-issued ID (e.g., driver license number, social security number, etc.) or a randomly generated number. A computational binding commitment to this ID is used in the BLE messaged generation algorithm. If the user is tested positive for COVID-19, the commitment can be used to prevent a malicious change or replacement of the keys after the commitment.

8) Performance: Our design is limited by multiple real-world operational Constraints:

1) **Short messages:** BLE communication enables each phone to send only relatively short messages. For efficiency and robustness, we require our messages to fit inside the payload of one BLE message, i.e., 16 bytes of data.[3]
2) **Efficiency:** To reduce the performance and battery requirements of our solution, the application must use limited CPU resources. We therefore limit it to using only efficient symmetric key cryptography (AES and HMAC). Moreover, real time calculations, such as computing the ephemeral ID, use only AES rather than HMAC.
3) **Limited download channel:** A server run by the MoH will publish the information that is required to check for exposure to new COVID-19 infected people. Each copy of the application must download this data, but we can only expect users to download a few megabytes of data per day. We limit the size of the data to approximately 5 MBytes for 1000 new COVID-19 positive persons per day. Our design supports *dynamic* trade-off between the length of the linkabilty period and size of the contact updates. Increasing this period from one hour to one day allows us to support 24000 new COVID-19 positive persons per day with the same 5 MBytes size.
4) **Run time of exposure detection algorithm:**The complexity of the algorithm that checks for exposure is linear in the number of BLE messages received and number of COVID-19 positive persons.

III. Cryptographic Design

In this section we will describe some central technical points in our cryptogarphic design. The full version with the detailed cryptographic design can be found in the full specification of the system [10].

A. Key Derivation

We divide the time to days, and each day to epochs of T_E minutes. We suggest setting $T_E = 60$ and therefore a day has 24 epochs. We further divide the time to units of T_U minutes, and suggest using $T_U = 5$. Each device will change the ephemeral ID that it sends every T_U minutes. (The reason for changing the ephemeral ID more frequently than changing the epoch is to prevent linkage between different ephemeral IDs that a user sends in the same epoch, unless the user is later diagnosed as COVID-19 positive.)

We use a tree-like key derivation scheme. The goal is to allow the server to broadcast separate keys for each epoch. This makes it much harder to link messages of the same infected person across different epochs. However, the scheme also allows the server to broadcast daily keys for reducing the total bandwidth.

We chose to derive all keys in two steps, first deriving daily keys from the master key, and from these daily keys deriving epoch keys. This allows the server to store the daily or epoch keys in a lexicographic order, without information that allows to link contacts across different days or epochs. Note that from a privacy perspective it is always preferable to only store epoch keys. However, we support the option of storing and sending daily keys in case that the of number of infected persons is large and it is required to optimizing the bandwidth.

The key derivation tree is depicted in Figure 1. Due to the page limit we do not provide here the full description of the key derivation process, and refer the user to the full version of this paper or to our cryptographic specification in [10].

Design Intuition: The key $PreK^{i,j}_{\text{epoch}}$ is derived from the day key. The key $K^{i,j}_{\text{epoch}}$ is derived from $PreK^{i,j}_{\text{epoch}}$ using the key K^{i}_{com} which binds the keys to a unique ID value. On the other hand, we do not want to require the server to broadcast K^{i}_{com} to users since this value will enable them to connect values sent by an infected person in different epochs. Therefore we derive $K^{i,j}_{\text{epoch}}$ from $PreK^{i,j}_{\text{epoch}}$, and have the server only broadcast $K^{i,j}_{\text{epoch}}$ to users. The keys $K^{i,j}_{\text{epochENC}}$ and $K^{i,j}_{\text{epochMAC}}$ are derived from $K^{i,j}_{\text{epoch}}$. These keys will be used by users to verify that the BLE message they received corresponds to a infected person. The key $K^{i,j}_{\text{epochVER}}$ will be used to ensure that only users which receive the ephemeral ID can reconstruct a "proof" which depends on this key. This value verifies to the server that the user indeed received this BLE message from a COVID-19 positive person.

B. Ephemeral IDs

We first list the rational for the design that we suggest:

1) The ephemeral ID should include an authenticated encryption of the location of the transmitting device. This is required in order to prevent relay attacks that broadcast the ephemeral ID to users in other locations. The design must also prevent attacks where the relay changes the original ephemeral ID, for example by xoring values to the ciphertext in order to change the original encrypted location to another location.

[3]Some of the other projects use the same message length, for example the Privacy-Preserving Contact Tracing project of Apple and Google.

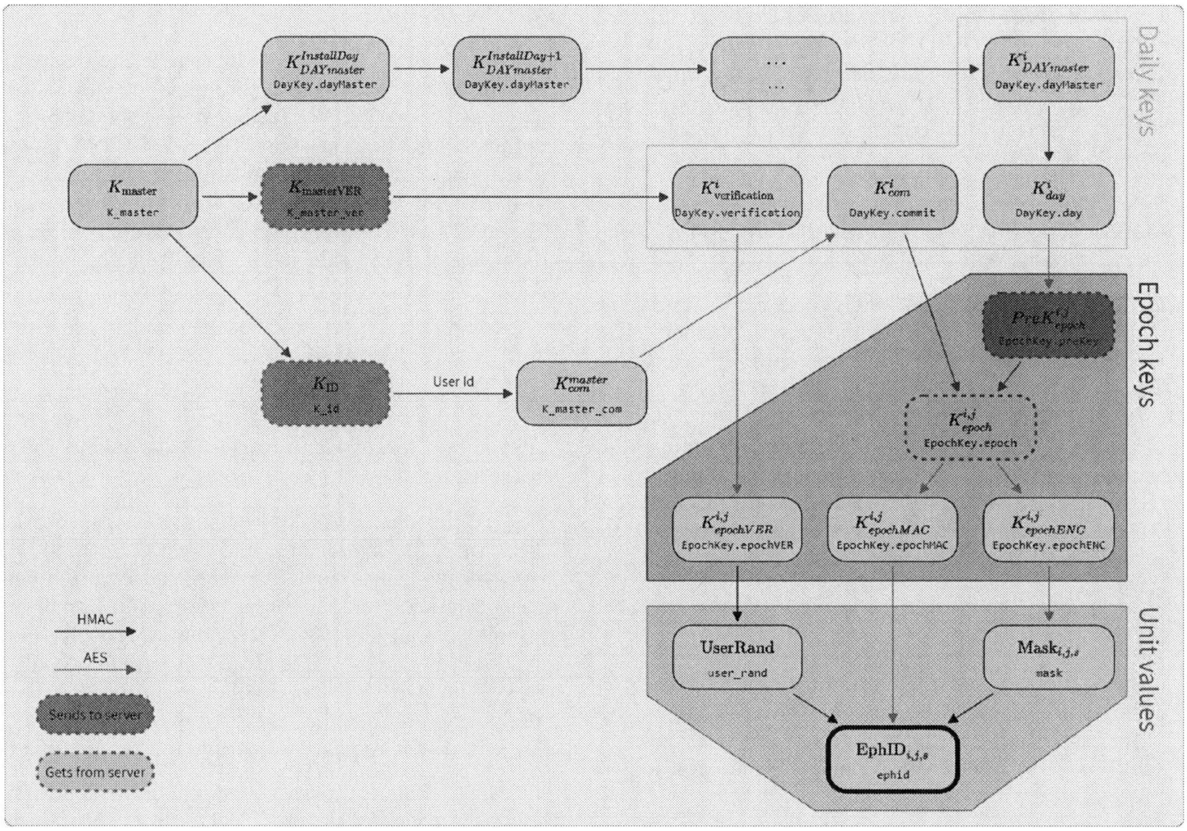

Fig. 1: The key derivation mechanism.

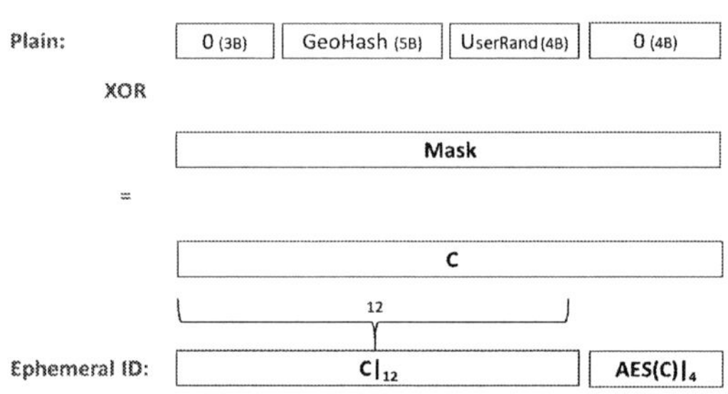

Fig. 2: The derivation of the Ephemeral ID.

2) There is a constraint of sending only 16 bytes in the ephemeral ID.
3) Another constraint is that the computation must be quick, since it must be run in real time (unlike the key derivations). Therefore we prefer using AES to using HMAC.
4) Checking at the client side for physical contacts, should be run in time which is linear in the number of infected persons and the number of recorded beacons.

The derivation of the Ephemeral ID described in Figure 2. The ephemeral ID for time unit s in epoch j of day i is a 16 byte value that is generated in the following method. The application sets a random 4 byte value, UserRand, as a truncation of the epoch verification key $K^{i,j}_{\mathrm{epochVER}}$. It also computes a 5 byte GeoHash of its current location. It then runs the following computation.

$$\mathrm{Mask_{i,j,s}} = \mathrm{AES}(\mathrm{K^{i,j}_{epochENC}}, \mathrm{s})$$
$$\mathrm{UserRand} = \mathrm{Truncate}(\mathrm{K^{i,j}_{epochVER}}, 4)$$
$$\mathrm{Plain_{i,j,s}} = 0\ (3B)\ ||\ \mathrm{GeoHash}\ (5B)\ ||\ \mathrm{UserRand}\ (4B)\ ||\ 0\ (4B)$$
$$\mathrm{C_{i,j,s}} = \mathrm{Plain_{i,j,s}} \oplus \mathrm{Mask_{i,j,s}}$$
$$\mathrm{EphID_{i,j,s}} = \mathrm{Truncate}(\mathrm{C_{i,j,s}}, 12)\ ||$$
$$\quad \mathrm{Truncate}(\mathrm{AES}(\mathrm{K^{i,j}_{epochMAC}}, \mathrm{C_{i,j,s}}), 4)$$

A note on UserRand: The UserRand field is used to enable the receiver of the ephemeral ID to prove that it received this message. Ideally, this message would be unique per ephemeral ID, for example computed as $\mathrm{Truncate}(\mathrm{AES}(\mathrm{K^{i,j}_{epochVER}}, \mathrm{s}), 4)$. However, since the ephemeral ID is generated in real time, we prefer to improve the latency of this operation and use the same UserRand value for all ephemeral IDs sent in an epoch. This will enable the receiver to prove that it received an ephemeral ID in this epoch, but not the exact time and number of ephemeral IDs received.

MAC size: Due to communication constraints, our MAC

is only 32-bits long. However, we assume that for deciding on exposure, the application will require at least two valid ephemeral IDs in a short time interval. And that means that in most cases, a relay attacker needs to forge two or more messages, and that will happen with a negligible probability of approximately 2^{-64}.

A note on GPS information accuracy and availability: We propose sending only coarse geo-location information (e.g., accuracy of ± 500 meters). We believe this is sufficient to prevent most cases of relay attacks, without compromising the users' privacy (Bluetooth range is much less than 500 meters). As location information might not be available (e.g., a long tunnel, location is disabled by the user, etc.), the information encoding should allow notifying that no location information is available (e.g., all zero bytes).

A note on the storing the GPS information: The Geo-Hash, which encodes the location, need not be kept secret from the receiver of the BLE message, since the receiver is physically close to the sender. Moreover, we assume that the phone may record its own GPS information. However, one can be worried that external access to the data stored on the device (for example by compromising the device, or using a court order), will reveal the location data. It would have therefore been preferable for the device to store a MAC of the geo-location, keyed by a key which is sent in the ephemeral ID and deleted afterwards. However, the current length of the ephemeral ID does not support a solution of this type.

C. *Communication with the Ministry of Health and Checking for Exposure*

For full details about the process of uploading keys to the MoH by COVID-19 positive persons, key broadcast, and local check for exposure see the full specification of the system [10].

IV. Deployment

A BLE-based contact tracing application, Hamagen 2, was deployed by the Israel Ministry of Health in late July (see source code at https://github.com/MohGovIL/rn-contact-tracing). This application was an update to a previous version of the application, Hamagen 1, which was based on GPS location data. Hamagen 1 initially had a very large number of downloads, but as time passed a large percentage of its users stopped using it. Unfortunately, the deployment of Hamagen 2 was a failure, and very few people chose to use it on a regular basis. We can identify two major reasons for this failure: technical issues, and trust issues.

a) Technical issues: The application suffered from various usability issues, especially in the first versions after the initial release. The issues included high battery consumption on some phones, and lack of support for older and some new phones. Bluetooth connection with other devices was also affected in some cases. These issues arose from two main reasons:

1) The release date was determined by a government resolution, without providing time for beta testing. The application was only briefly tested by a small group of developers on about 30 devices. The next step was releasing the application to more than a million users.
2) Apple and Google prevented the MoH from using the GAEN API. The application developers had to bypass the various limitation on BLE-based contact tracing without the OS support. The Israeli MoH decided that location data is needed in order to support location-based tracing of contacts with people who do not use smartphones. (In Israel, a large percentage of the population does not use smartphones for religious reasons, and the GAEN API does not provide a solution for them.) Although this unique local issue was explained to Apple and Google, they did not agree to change their global restriction on using GPS location together with the GAEN API.

b) Trust issues: Even taking into consideration the technical difficulties, we argue that the main reason for the failure of the deployment was the lack of trust among the general public. The implementation followed our design and was endorsed by prominent privacy advocates, but this fact was not communicated to the public. Moreover, since the beginning of the pandemic, Israel has been trying to trace contacts using intrusive surveillance technology of the Israel Security Agency. Without adequate publicity, which was lacking, the public was unable to distinguish between that type of surveillance, and the privacy-preserving design of Hamagen 2. In addition, people also had a general distrust for the government's response to COVID-19. As a result, people were reluctant to install any application that, in their view, might be spying on them.

While we lack professional expertise in this area, we believe that if the public had trusted the effectiveness and privacy of the contact tracing solution, many people would have used it despite the technical difficulties. Therefore, trust issues were the primary reason for the failure of the application deployment.

Acknowledgment

We thank the many researchers with whom we discussed the design, including Manuel Barbosa, Eli Biham, Dan Boneh, Yehuda Lindell, Moni Naor, and Adi Shamir. We are very grateful for Ron Asherov and other contributors for their hard work on the Python reference implementation and helpful comments.

This work was supported by the BIU Center for Research in Applied Cryptography and Cyber Security in conjunction with the Israel National Cyber Bureau in the Prime Minister's Office, by the Alter Family Foundation, and by Len Blavatnik and the Blavatnik Family foundation. Eyal Ronen is a member of CPIIS.

References

[1] Apple and Google. Exposure notification cryptography specification, April 2020. https://www.apple.com/covid19/contacttracing/.

[2] Lars Baumgärtner, Alexandra Dmitrienko, Bernd Freisleben, Alexander Gruler, Jonas Höchst, Joshua Kühlberg, Mira Mezini, Markus Miettinen, Anel Muhamedagic, Thien Duc Nguyen, Alvar Penning, Dermot Frederik Pustelnik, Filipp Roos, Ahmad-Reza Sadeghi, Michael Schwarz, and Christian Uhl. Mind the GAP: security & privacy risks of contact tracing apps. *CoRR*, abs/2006.05914, 2020.

[3] Ran Canetti, Yael Tauman Kalai, Anna Lysyanskaya, Ronald L. Rivest, Adi Shamir, Emily Shen, Ari Trachtenberg, Mayank Varia, and Daniel J. Weitzner. Privacy-preserving automated exposure notification. Cryptology ePrint Archive, Report 2020/863, 2020. https://eprint.iacr.org/2020/863.

[4] Paul-Olivier Dehaye and Joel Reardon. Swisscovid: a critical analysis of risk assessment by swiss authorities, 2020.

[5] Gary F. Hatke, Monica Montanari, Swaroop Appadwedula, Michael Wentz, John Meklenburg, Louise Ivers, Jennifer Watson, and Paul Fiore. Using bluetooth low energy (BLE) signal strength estimation to facilitate contact tracing for COVID-19, 2020.

[6] Archanaa S. Krishnan, Yaling Yang, and Patrick Schaumont. Risk and architecture factors in digital exposure notification. Cryptology ePrint Archive, Report 2020/582, 2020. https://eprint.iacr.org/2020/582.

[7] Joseph K. Liu, Man Ho Au, Tsz Hon Yuen, Cong Zuo, Jiawei Wang, Amin Sakzad, Xiapu Luo, and Li Li. Privacy-preserving covid-19 contact tracing app: A zero-knowledge proof approach. Cryptology ePrint Archive, Report 2020/528, 2020. https://eprint.iacr.org/2020/528.

[8] Singapore Ministry of Health and Government Technology Agency. TraceTogether, 2020. https://www.tracetogether.gov.sg/.

[9] Krzysztof Pietrzak. Delayed authentication: Preventing replay and relay attacks in private contact tracing. *IACR Cryptol. ePrint Arch.*, 2020:418, 2020.

[10] Benny Pinkas and Eyal Ronen. Hashomer – a proposal for a privacy-preserving bluetooth based contact tracing scheme for Hamagen, 2020. https://github.com/eyalr0/HashomerCryptoRef/blob/master/documents/hashomer.pdf.

[11] Leonie Reichert, Samuel Brack, and Björn Scheuermann. A survey of automatic contact tracing approaches. Cryptology ePrint Archive, Report 2020/672, 2020. https://eprint.iacr.org/2020/672.

[12] Carmela Troncoso, Mathias Payer, Jean-Pierre Hubaux, Marcel Salathé, James R. Larus, Edouard Bugnion, Wouter Lueks, Theresa Stadler, Apostolos Pyrgelis, Daniele Antonioli, Ludovic Barman, Sylvain Chatel, Kenneth G. Paterson, Srdjan Capkun, David A. Basin, Jan Beutel, Dennis Jackson, Marc Roeschlin, Patrick Leu, Bart Preneel, Nigel P. Smart, Aysajan Abidin, Seda F. Gürses, Michael Veale, Cas Cremers, Michael Backes, Nils Ole Tippenhauer, Reuben Binns, Ciro Cattuto, Alain Barrat, Dario Fiore, Manuel Barbosa, Rui Oliveira, and José Pereira. Decentralized privacy-preserving proximity tracing. *CoRR*, abs/2005.12273, 2020.

[13] Serge Vaudenay. Centralized or decentralized? the contact tracing dilemma. Cryptology ePrint Archive, Report 2020/531, 2020. https://eprint.iacr.org/2020/531.

[14] Zhiguo Wan and Xiaotong Liu. Contactchaser: A simple yet effective contact tracing scheme with strong privacy. Cryptology ePrint Archive, Report 2020/630, 2020. https://eprint.iacr.org/2020/630.

Towards Defeating Mass Surveillance and SARS-CoV-2: The Pronto-C2 Fully Decentralized Automatic Contact Tracing System

Gennaro Avitabile*, Vincenzo Botta†, Vincenzo Iovino‡ and Ivan Visconti§
DIEM, University of Salerno
Italy
Email: *gavitabile@unisa.it, †vbotta@unisa.it, ‡viovino@unisa.it, §visconti@unisa.it

Abstract—**Automatic contact tracing is currently used in several countries in order to limit the spread of SARS-CoV-2. Many governments decided to develop smartphone apps based on the "Exposure Notifications" designed by Apple and Google according to a decentralized approach previously proposed by the DP-3T team. Decentralization was pushed as a key feature to protect privacy in contrast to centralized approaches that could leverage automatic contact tracing to realize mass-surveillance programs.**

In this work, taking into account the privacy and integrity vulnerabilities of DP-3T systems, we show the design of a decentralized contact tracing system named Pronto-C2 that has better resilience against various attacks. We also discuss the significant overhead of Pronto-C2 when used in real-world scenarios.

I. Introduction

The COVID-19 pandemic is currently affecting daily life of many citizens in the world. People are forced to stay home for several weeks; uncertainty, sadness, economic downturn, unemployment, and restrictions on daily activities generate an impelling desire to join any government effort to stop as soon as possible the spread of the virus.

Following recommendations of epidemiologists [13], governments are proposing the use of smartphone applications to allow automatic contact tracing (ACT) of citizens. This raises the question of whether this digital form of contact tracing can be a subtle weapon for governments to violate the privacy of their citizens contributing to new and more sophisticated mass surveillance programs. The vast majority of ACT systems propose the use Bluetooth Low Energy (BLE) to estimate the distance. Among those, many ACT systems (e.g., DP-3T[1], MIT-PACT, UW-PACT and GAEN, the Apple&Google exposure notification system) follow a decentralized approach and claim to guarantee better privacy properties compared to centralized approaches (e.g., ROBERT or NTK).

[1]We say DP-3T to refer to systems proposed by the DP-3T team.

Workshop on Secure IT Technologies against COVID-19 (CoronaDef) 2021
21 February 2021, Virtual
https://dx.doi.org/10.14722/coronadef.2021.23013
www.ndss-symposium.org

Motivated by Snowden's revelations about previous attempts of governments to realize mass surveillance programs, in this paper we first analyze mass surveillance attacks that leverage weaknesses of automatic contact tracing systems. We focus in particular on DP-3T (still our analysis is significant also for many other decentralized ACT systems). Considering attacks proposed in recent literature, we discuss how a government can exploit the use of DP-3T to successfully mount privacy attacks contributing of a mass surveillance program. We show that privacy issues in DP-3T are not inherent in BLE-based contact tracing systems, contradicting a claim appeared in one of the documents published by the DP-3T team.

As main contribution of this work, we propose a different system named Pronto-C2 that, in our view, is more resilient against mass surveillance attacks. Pronto-C2 is based on a paradigm shift: instead of asking smartphones to send keys to the Big Brother (this corresponds to the approach of DP-3T), we construct a decentralized ACT system where smartphones anonymously and confidentially talk to each other in the presence of the Big Brother.

A. Related Work

Our work mainly focuses on proposing a new ACT system and evaluating its resilience to various attacks in comparison with DP-3T [11]. Still, the issues we discuss are significant to many other decentralized ACT systems such as MIT-PACT [17], UW-PACT [10] and TCN [22]. We remark that almost all vulnerabilities of DP-3T also apply at least in part to the currently widely used ACT systems based on GAEN [2].

DP-3T (and similar systems) exposes several vulnerabilities. Attacks can be carried out not only by the government, but also by unknown adversaries. These vulnerabilities have been explicitly mentioned in [10] (Section 3.1.3): *"This can be abused for surveillance purposes, but arguably, surveillance itself could be achieved by other methods"*.

Several vulnerabilities of DP-3T have been previously analyzed in various works [23], [24], [18], [21]. Vaudenay [23], [24] presented a detailed list of both privacy and integrity attacks against DP-3T; some of the attacks that we consider in this paper are indeed instantiations of the ones of Vaudenay, even though we give more emphasis to the possibility of exploiting such attacks for mass surveillance. The DP-3T team reacted to Vaudenay's work by presenting a public response to his attacks [12] that does not object on their applicability, and mainly tries to convey the message that those attacks are hard to mount and inherent to any decentralized approach. Our results show that the there can be systems that are resilient to those attacks.

Pietrzak [18] proposed solutions and mitigations to replay and relay attacks against DP-3T. In such attacks, one can inject false notifications of at-risk contacts. Furthermore, Pietrzak identified the issue that users of DP-3T can easily provide digital evidence of contacts with infected users. Another way of injecting false notifications is via bribing of the infected users, such an attack was conjectured to be applicable to decentralized systems like DP-3T by Vaudenay [24]. Avitabile et al. demonstrated several concrete instantiations of such attack with respect to GAEN-based ACT systems [4]. Tang [21] observed that DP-3T may be subject to identification attacks and presented a comprehensive survey on proximity tracing systems. Canetti et al. provided general formalizations of ACT systems [8], including one in the Universal Composability framework. According to these formalizations, the DP-3T and GAEN systems lack basic privacy and integrity properties.

There are several works providing practical evidence of the above mentioned vulnerabilities. In [20], Seiskari showed a proof-of-concept implementation of Vaudenay's Paparazzi attack [23], demonstrating that, in DP-3T, locations visited by infected users during the two weeks prior to their diagnosis can be tracked by any third party (not only the government) that can install a large fleet of BLE-sniffing devices. Notice that such devices can be completely passive (i.e., they do not broadcast an identifier beacon) and therefore not easily detectable. Baumgärtner et al. [5] provided empirical evidence for two important risks of the Apple&Google design, namely, as in DP-3T, tracing of infected users and replay/relay attacks.

An alternative approach to the above decentralized systems consists of giving more power to a server. Examples of such more centralized ACT systems are TraceTogether[1], adopted in Singapore and ROBERT [16] adopted in France. In [14] the authors reviewed both centralized and decentralized ACT systems such as DP-3T, NTK, and ROBERT, analyzing the different adversarial models and the corresponding risks.

Finally, some works proposed alternative ACT systems trying to improve integrity. Pinkas and Ronen [19], building upon a design similar to DP-3T, proposed a system with an improved resilience to relay attacks and a better verification of risks. Buccafurri et al. proposed an alternative protocol that completely avoids the exchange of identifier over BLE and instead relies on GPS[7].

Public-key cryptography. Like Pronto-C2 some systems leveraged public-key cryptography to offer better privacy guarantees. One of such systems is WeTrace[2][9] where public keys are exchanged over the BLE channel. An infected user A uploads messages encrypted with the public keys related to close contacts she had. These encrypted messages are independent of the public key A was broadcasting while being in contact with the recipients of the messages. While this might be beneficial for A's privacy, it can make easier to mount attacks generating false notifications of at risk contacts. Indeed, a user B may be alerted consequently to an upload performed by an infected user C who did not come into contact at all with B, but just received B's key trough other means.

Inria published on Github the design of a system named DESIRE [15] that uses the Diffie-Hellman protocol for key exchange. After being tested positive, a user uploads data related to the encounters he had during the previous days. Such data is computed by hashing the shared key along with an information depending on which of the two users is creating the report. This guarantees that if two users A and B have been in close proximity, and both of them end up being positive to SARS-CoV-2, they will send two different values to the server, making it impossible for the server itself to infer that A and B have been co-located. Differently from Pronto-C2, the at-risk status for each user is computed on a central server.

II. From DP-3T to GAEN

BLE allows smartphones physically close to each other to exchange identifiers requiring a low battery consumption. Such communication mechanism avoids GPS technology and third-party devices like Wi-Fi routers or base stations of cellular networks. In a BLE-based privacy-preserving ACT system after a short period of time each smartphone replaces the already announced pseudonym with a (seemingly independent) new one. Each smartphone receives pseudonyms sent by others and stores them locally. Therefore, a smartphone will have a database of both the announced and received pseudonyms. The central idea is that whenever a person is detected infected, smartphones that have been physically close to the smartphone of the infected person for a certain amount of time should show an alert to notify the potential at-risk contact. To realize this, the smartphone of the infected person should use the above database to reach out the smartphones that have recently been physically close to it. This communication is achieved through a backend server as follows. First, the smartphone of the infected person will use the above two databases to communicate data to the backend server. The server could run some computations on data received from smartphones of infected citizens. The server will also use collected/computed data to answer pull requests of smartphones that desire to check if there is any notification for them. Intuitively, the above approach guarantees some degree of privacy through the unlinkability of the pseudonyms. Nevertheless, the risk that such systems can be abused to violate privacy remains a major concern and can affect their adoption.

An important point of the design of a BLE-based ACT system is the generation of pseudonyms used by smartphones. Two major approaches have been proposed so far. In a centralized approach pseudonyms are generated by the server. Each smartphone, during the setup of the ACT smartphone application, connects to the server and receives its pseudonyms.

[2]We became aware of WeTrace only few months after first publishing our work on ePrint, informed by Adrienne Fichter.

Therefore the server knows all the pseudonyms honestly used in the system. This is pretty obviously a clear open door to mass surveillance. Such dangers are discussed in [11]. The decentralized approach breaks the obvious linkability of pseudonyms belonging to the same smartphone by letting the smartphone itself generate such pseudonyms.

One can trivially realize a decentralized BLE-based ACT system giving to the server the role of proxy that forwards to non-infected persons the pseudonyms of the infected individuals who decide to upload their pseudonyms[3] after being detected infected. Therefore, everyone, including the server, learns directly pseudonyms that have been used during the previous days by recently infected persons. On the other hand, the pseudonyms generated by smartphones belonging to non-infected persons are not uploaded to the server and remain visible only to whoever was physically close to those smartphones. Such decentralized systems seemingly have a potential to offer better privacy protection compared to known systems that use the centralized approach.

It is truly problematic to realize BLE-based privacy-preserving smartphone applications that can practically (in the sense of usability, battery consumption, and so on) work on (almost) all currently used BLE smartphones, unless some flexibility is allowed by Apple&Google through updates of iOS and Android. To this regard, Apple&Google have released updates of iOS and Android providing an application program interface for exposure notification (GAEN) [2]. The access to the API is restricted to specific smartphone apps authorized by Apple&Google (i.e., the apps selected by governments). Sadly, if one would like to implement a usable smartphone application (i.e., an app that runs in the background without battery drain on a very large percentage of the currently available smartphones) that rotates the BLE identifier beacon then it is hard to avoid the use of GAEN and therefore the app must use their approach for pseudonym generation and exposition, inheriting the related limitations/vulnerabilities.

This lack of flexibility generates some interesting consequences. First of all, the centralized approach is hard to implement since it relies on pseudonyms generated by the server and then advertised in the BLE identifier beacon by the smartphone. However, the generation of pseudonyms can only happen inside the smartphone when using GAEN. Such mismatch implies that the decision of Apple&Google makes harder to realize the centralized approach and any other different system (even an alternative decentralized one) that relies on generating BLE identifier beacons in a different way.

III. Privacy Issues in DP-3T Protocols

Starting with the attacks presented by Vaudenay [23], we discuss the privacy issues in DP-3T. In some of the attacks a government through its natural power controls (even partially) the server, the laboratories that detect infections and the national territory to violate privacy, possibly to collect more data, and use them in mass surveillance programs.

[3]The actual information uploaded is a seed that generates the pseudonyms.

A major privacy problem is that in DP-3T (and all analogue systems) one can be traced even when walking alone. Indeed, a passive antenna can detect a pseudonym without transmitting anything (we name this *silent tracing*), and can later on check if it belongs to the list of infected persons. It is easy to link the real identity of an infected person with the pseudonyms she has been using. Such antennas can be installed nearby any place where the citizen can be identified, and this allows to connect pseudonyms to identities. Concretely, the key weakness of DP-3T is that asking smartphone applications to hand over the used keys/pseudonyms to the server is like asking infected citizens to kneel down in front of the Big Brother.

IV. A Decentralized Alternative: Pronto-C2

As main contribution of this work, we present Pronto-C2, a new decentralized privacy-preserving ACT system based on BLE. Pronto-C2 can be implemented through government servers but also can be fully decentralized using blockchain technology. Full decentralization can play an important role in ACT systems since many citizens may prefer to use their smartphones only when systems are transparent and resilient to integrity attacks, in addition to being privacy preserving.

Our decentralized solution relies on a paradigm shift compared to the approach of DP-3T. Indeed, instead of asking infected people to hand over their keys to the Big Brother, we allow citizens to anonymously and confidentially call each other in the presence of the Big Brother.

Diffie and Hellman proposed a key exchange protocol (i.e., the DH protocol) where two parties can establish a secret key K by just sending one message each on a public channel. In our view, the most natural way to realize a privacy-preserving ACT system consists of having as pseudonym a group element that corresponds to a message in the DH protocol. To actually realize such form of ACT system, one needs to solve the following two main problems.

Anonymous call: realizing a mechanism that allows an infected party to use K in order to call the other party in a secure and privacy-preserving way.

Shortening pseudonyms: making sure that the size of a group element fits the number of available bits in a BLE identifier beacon.

Calling (anonymously) the infected person. We solve the first problem by asking the infected party, after having received a proper authorization from the laboratory that detected the infection, to upload K along with the authorization to a bulletin board. The bulletin board can be just managed by a server as in DP-3T, but ideally it should be implemented through a decentralized blockchain so that we can decentralize the server, making the entire process transparent and reliable.

When implementing the bulletin board with a blockchain, the verification of the authorization must be performed by a smart contact and thus the check should be accomplished uniquely with public information. For this reason, we suggest the use of digital signatures. To make the upload of K unlinkable with the real identity of the infected person, we suggest the use of blind signatures. The basic idea is that laboratories receive from the government some unpredictable activation codes that are then one by one given to infected persons. Then, an infected person connects to a service in order to exchange the authorization code with some blind signatures that will be useful to then upload on the bulletin board data associated to calls. In case of use of a blockchain to implement the bulletin board, this exchange of an authorization code with a blind signature is performed off-chain since the server will use a signature secret key, and thus it cannot be directly implemented by a smart contract.

Notice that the approach of Pronto-C2 is completely different from the one of DP-3T. Indeed, while in DP-3T the pseudonyms of the infected person are broadcast to everyone, we instead ask the infected party to send a message that is understandable uniquely by the party with which she was in close proximity. Therefore, K is more similar to a phone call where the infected party sends to the answering party the following message:[4] "Hello, it is you that were next to me... and I've just discovered that I'm infected".

Every person that is not infected will connect to the server (or to the blockchain) and will download the recently uploaded keys to search for K (data don't need to be stored, the search can happen while downloading data). Notice that there is a different key K to check for every BLE identifier beacon received in the last two weeks that has not been already discovered. This step should be preferably performed while the phone is connected to the charger and to a Wi-Fi network. Moreover, for those cases where the daily amount of data to download is excessive, one could specify target states/regions in the country, so that only a restricted amount of information needs to be managed. In this case, a call would also specify a corresponding state/region. In addition to K, the infected person can also upload some auxiliary information (e.g., about BLE signal) to improve risk scoring or to share data with epidemiologists.

We remark that avoiding that two smartphones with pseudonyms A and B upload the same K (this would leak some –most likely irrelevant – information), is straightforward: A could just upload $H(K||A||B)$ while B could just upload $H(K||B||A)$, where H is a cryptographic hash function.

Shortening pseudonyms. Current standards suggest to use at least 256 bits for a group element to safely run the DH protocol over elliptic curves. This size, however, exceeds the space available in a BLE identifier beacon. One might think to resolve the issue of the small space in a BLE identifier beacon by just resorting to very short (and therefore in our view too risky in case of mass surveillance attacks) keys or by splitting the information into multiple identifier beacons that rotate quickly. We instead propose a different approach that allows to use many bits for the group element while still remaining with one identifier beacon only. We decouple the group element from the pseudonym precisely like in operating systems a large amount of data is represented by a pointer. Recall that a value announced in a BLE identifier beacon should last only for a few minutes, to then be replaced by a new one. The smartphone will periodically generate new independent group elements for DH and will keep them locally. Since they are too large to be sent in BLE identifier beacons, the smartphone will upload them to a bulletin board. Again, our design is flexible and the bulletin board can be maintained by a server or alternatively be implemented with a blockchain. Notice that this generation of group elements is done only once in a while, and therefore can typically be performed when the smartphone is on charge and is connected to a Wi-Fi network.

Silent tracing. Pronto-C2 is clearly secure with respect to silent tracing. In fact, it is based on virtual anonymous calls originated from a recently detected infected person, and addressed to whoever has been in close proximity with her. Indeed, when a person walks alone and passes by a silent tracing device, the sole transmission of the pseudonym used in that moment by the smartphone does not allow to understand if later on that person is infected. In fact, there will be no key K that can be found in the list of virtual anonymous calls.

Shameless tracing. A government can also try to trace citizens by having on its territory many devices that behave as smartphones, therefore announcing pseudonyms with the hope of receiving a call or making calls in order to infer some information on the locations and identities of the citizens. It goes without saying that such attack is easier to detect compared to silent tracing. Indeed, the smartphone application could easily inform the owner at any time on the number of BLE identifier beacons that are currently received. Therefore, there is more room for citizens to realize the existence of malicious devices and ask police to destroy them and to identify the criminals that were trying to abuse the ACT system. Any government that would like to save its reputation convincing citizens to still use the smartphone application should take severe actions against such criminals. Obviously, if there is no prompt reaction of the government then citizens will feel that some attempts of mass surveillance are in progress and will simply switch off the smartphone application.

Pronto-C2 is secure against shameless tracing. Indeed, even though with shameless tracing the attacker will receive calls from an infected user, the calls are not linkable and the infected citizen remains hidden among all other infected citizens.

Side-channel attacks. As in all ACT systems, users could be de-anonymized through the IP address when connecting to servers. Moreover, when uploading a batch of group elements some attention should be paid so that they are not linkable. We therefore suggest the use of artificial delays and uploads of bogus data with the only purpose to confuse and make harder to achieve any profiling attempt. Furthermore, we suggest also a simple solution to mitigate such linkability problems which consists of allowing each user to select her own favorite mixer. Such mixer can be selected among several options that can belong to heterogeneous entities (e.g., political parties, large organizations defending civil rights). By doing so, users could pick their favorite options to protect their IP addresses when uploading their pseudonyms and their anonymous calls

[4]"Pronto" stays for "Hello" and C2 pronounced in English stands for "it is you" in Neapolitan language, as in the title of a song by Nino D'Angelo.

to the bulletin board. Moreover, the user can send batches of pseudonyms and calls since they will be mixed by the mixer that will also apply some artificial delays and dummy traffic, thus guaranteeing some level of unlinkability. We give a more detailed description of this idea in Section V. We stress that ACT systems currently deployed are at least in part affected by such issues and somehow ignore them. Still, we prefer to discuss possible workarounds, even though they obviously introduce extra overhead. DoS attacks can be mitigated with standard approaches (e.g., CAPTCHAs, proofs of work, anonymous tokens).

Remark on the "Paparazzi" attack of [23] and the DP-3T answer [12]. Vaudenay in [23] showed a privacy attack to DP-3T proposing an antenna that can be used to eavesdrop the identifier beacons sent by smartphones. The DP-3T team answered to [23] in [12] claiming that "This is a known attack vector inherent to all contact tracing systems, whether centralized or decentralized (SRE, Inherent Risk 1)". Our ACT system Pronto-C2 contradicts this claim. It might be that the DP-3T team was implicitly referring only to systems that follow their decentralized approach. This would imply that Apple&Google provides through GAEN a system that is inherently affected by non-inherent attacks to privacy.

V. Performance of Pronto-C2

In this section we describe how Pronto-C2 could be used in concrete scenarios and analyze its performance. We remark that one should not think that an ACT system must perform well in all possible scenarios in order to be considered. The sole fact that in some countries the performance of an ACT system is good enough makes the system of practical relevance and worthy to study. Pronto-C2 could be a viable solution in some countries, but it might not be efficient enough in others.

Pronto-C2 involves the following actors: the user U, who runs the smartphone application; the server Server, that manages the bulletin board; the medical laboratory HA; the authentication service AuthService.

There is a risk that U is subject to linkability/deanonymization attacks due to timings and IP addresses of the TLS connections with Server when uploading or downloading data. Such attacks also affect DP-3T, and in general are applicable to any system if no specific countermeasure is used. One might consider onion routing and mix networks to protect U against such attacks, but the impact on performance remains unclear. In order to give a fair description of a practical realization of Pronto-C2, we do not ignore this issue and we therefore include here a mitigation based on mixers. We will consider a setting where U can freely select a mixer MixServer that she trusts, and mixers do not need to be approved by the government, they can be spontaneously run by anyone.

Server owns a pair of private and public keys $(\mathsf{sk}_{\mathsf{Server}}, \mathsf{pk}_{\mathsf{Server}})$ of a public key encryption scheme (e.g., ElGamal instantiated on the elliptic curve used for the key exchange), the public key of Server is made publicly available at set-up time. Every time U has to send data to Server, U will actually encrypt the data with $\mathsf{pk}_{\mathsf{Server}}$ and send the resulting ciphertexts to MixServer. A mixer waits for enough data to be collected, and then performs a mixing and sends them to Server. In addition, MixServer can also download all data from Server so that U can use MixServer also to retrieve anonymous calls and ephemeral keys.

There can be several heterogeneous mixers available, provided by large institutions like no-profit organizations, political parties, national/state/local governments, as well as several smaller mixers that can serve a district, a school, a group of friends/relatives. U will obviously choose the one that he trusts more in performing properly the service with a sufficiently large amount of collected data and without abusing it. It remains possible for a user to ignore this suggestion and to use some proper delays and then sending the encrypted data directly to Server through onion routing and/or relying on the partial hiding provided by mobile operators and public Wi-Fi networks (somehow they can also be seen as light forms of mixers). We will continue our discussion considering the case of a citizen using a mixer that she trusts.

Server works as a bulletin board, so all data ever received by Server are made publicly available after being decrypted. HA is the laboratory that perform the SARS-CoV-2 tests. If a user U gets tested positive, HA hands U an authorization code Code. AuthService is the service in charge of authorizing users to upload anonymous calls to the bulletin board. It can also be useful to issue credentials to upload ephemeral keys to the bulletin board, in order to mitigate DoS attacks.

Each user U executes the following operations preferably when the smartphone is connected to a battery charger, and preferably having Internet access via Wi-Fi[5]:

- U generates a set of 96 ephemeral and secret keys to be used for the next day (there is a rotation every 15 minutes).
- U connects to AuthService to prove to be a legitimate user of the system needing to announce new pseudonyms. With this connection, U obtains 96 blind signatures of the generated ephemeral keys. This step is needed to avoid DoS attacks on the bulletin board.
- U uploads the ephemeral keys to the bulletin board. U encrypts the 96 ephemeral keys, along with the related unblinded signatures, and sends the resulting ciphertexts to MixServer that, after having collected a sufficiently large amount of data, mixes and sends them to Server who will eventually decrypt and publish them. U will obtain the addresses of his ephemeral keys by querying Server with the first l bits (the value of l will be discussed later) of each key. Server will return, for each query, all the ephemeral keys that match these bits, along with the addresses of such keys. U will store the addresses of his ephemeral keys and will broadcast them during the following day. By doing so, U is able to efficiently retrieve his addresses while hiding the link between them to Server since each query corresponds to a fairly large

[5]We implicitly assume that all TCP/IP connections use TLS.

set of ephemeral keys. To add more noise, dummy queries may also be performed.

- U downloads from Server (this step could also be performed through MixServer that can have a local copy of data available on Server) the ephemeral keys $\mathsf{Eph}_{\mathsf{U}_i}$ for all addr_i collected during the day by querying Server (or MixServer) with the first l bits of each address collected during the day. For each query, U will receive a set of ephemeral keys and U can select the needed key.
- U downloads from Server (as above this step could also be performed through MixServer) all the calls that have been added to the bulletin board after U performed the last download of the calls (e.g., the previous day). Consequently, U evaluates his contagion risk.
- If U is positive to SARS-CoV-2, U receives Code from HA who delivered him the diagnosis.
- The infected user U computes the anonymous call for each ephemeral key received, optionally excluding the ones encountered at a specific time or date, and connects to AuthService to obtain a blind signature for each call. This is done by asking AuthService to sign one call at a time. Notice that the government knows the identities of infected citizens, therefore there is no need of special protection in this step.
- The infected user U encrypts the calls along with the unblinded signatures, with $\mathsf{pk}_{\mathsf{Server}}$. Then, U uploads these data via MixServer, as done for the upload of the ephemeral keys. If U feels uncomfortable in giving evidence of being infected to MixServer, U can send dummy encrypted calls on a daily basis (i.e., whenever U uploads new ephemeral keys).

Note that Pronto-C2 will behave exactly as in DP-3T regarding data sent during the day over the BLE channel (e.g., it will send and receive the same amount of data without performing additional computations).

To give an idea of the overall performance, we report an example of a concrete execution in a typical scenario. To analyze the performance, we take into account the memory usage of the smartphone application, the amount of uploaded and downloaded data, and the number of exponentiations the smartphone has to execute. We assume that: each user U has 100 contacts per day on average; there are on average 5000 new infected individuals per day within a single country; U uses a new pseudonym every 15 minutes; the contagion time window is 10 days long; the dummy calls produced by the user are 100 per day on average; there are 5 million users that upload their ephemeral keys each day; we set $l = 17$. By doing so the resulting set of ephemeral keys would be of about 3663 elements on average. [6]. In the same scenario, if l is equal to 10, the number of ephemeral keys that is downloaded by each user to compute the anonymous calls is 468750 on average, while, increasing l to 25 the number of ephemeral keys downloaded is 15. In general, the number of downloaded keys is the total number of ephemeral keys published divided by 2 to the number of bits fixed in the prefix. Compared to l equale to 15, in case l is equal to 10 the requests of the user are hidden in a larger number of calls, while in case l is equal to 25 the number of ephemeral keys downloaded by U is smaller and it is easier for an adversary to guess which ephemeral key was searched by U.

Every smartphone has to maintain on the local memory less than 150KB. We did not count the space required by blind signatures since they are sent to MixServer and erased as soon as they are received from AuthService.

By using blind signatures based on RSA [6] with a length of 2048 bits for the modulus, the size of downloaded data is about 177MB[7]. The vast majority of daily downloaded data comes from the anonymous calls needed to evaluate the infection risk and their size is about 153MB, that can be processed as soon as received and deleted immediately after that, without flooding the memory of the smartphone. Downloading 177MB could be expensive in terms of rate plan, therefore we recommend to perform this operation when the smartphone is connected to a Wi-Fi connection. Furthermore, governments, cooperating with mobile operators, could reduce or eliminate such costs. In this way, users who do not have access to a Wi-Fi connection would be able to benefit from the service anyway, obviously limiting the use of MixServer to the steps that are more critical for privacy protection.

The amount of daily uploaded data is less than 350KB if the user is not infected. An infected user uploads also about 250KB daily.

The smartphone computes one exponentiation for each blind signature. In order to get an ElGamal encryption the smartphone computes 2 exponentiations for each 32 bytes of plain-text data.

On daily basis there are about 2000 exponentiations for dummy calls and the total number of exponentiations needed to store all the ephemeral keys is around 1100.

Also there are daily 100 exponentiations to risk of contagion. Therefore, the total number of exponentiations computed on average per day by a smartphone of a non-infected user is below 3500. If the user is tested positive to SARS-CoV-2, the number of additional exponentiations he performs is 10000.

VI. Attacks, Analysis and Comparison

We consider the following attacks.

Paparazzi attack: Adv controls a fleet of passive BLE devices (i.e., they receive messages but do not transmit) placed in locations that are known to him. Adv traces the movements of the infected users during the contagion time window.
This attack is not applicable to Pronto-C2 since different ephemeral keys (i.e., pseudonyms) generated by the same user U are not linkable. Adv could try to track a target infected user U exploiting the calls available on the bulletin board. Since the

[6] l can be chosen dynamically considering the number of ephemeral keys that have been added that day and ensuring that the size of the set of keys allows for an efficient search while providing sufficient privacy.

[7] Even if the amount of downloaded data can seem considerable, it is worth noting that when using a video streaming application (e.g., YouTube), smartphones typically download very large amounts of data.

devices used by Adv are passive, no calls of U will ever be directed to Adv. The only way for Adv to track U is to extract the ephemeral keys used to generate the calls and associate them to a single user. Since the calls are anonymously sent to Server, Adv fails in linking together the calls of U.

Orwell attack: the attack is analogous to Paparazzi but Adv now also receives all data that is in possession of the Server. This attack is not applicable to Pronto-C2. Assuming that the upload of the calls on the bulletin board is performed through an anonymous channel, in order to link these calls, Adv needs to discover which call was blinded by U before obtaining the corresponding signature from AuthService. This would require Adv to break the blindness property of the blind signature. Even if Adv breaks the blindness of the signature scheme, the additional information received is the set of calls sent to Server by U, but none of them is a call that Adv understands. Indeed, none of the passive devices controlled by Adv is the recipient of a call. Adv would need to take all the pairs of ephemeral keys recorded by each passive device D_i, and try to compute a call between the two users that owns these two ephemeral keys. If the computed call is equal to a call published by U, then Adv knows that U was located in proximity to D_i. However, if Adv is able to successfully compute a call starting from two ephemeral identifiers, it is easy to show that Adv can be used to define an adversary breaking the DH assumption.

Matrix attack: Adv is as in the Orwell attack in terms of the information he has access to. On the other hand, Adv's devices can actively send messages over the BLE channel. Adv combines data in his possession with the ability to actively send messages of the contact tracing protocol over the BLE channel in order to trace infected citizens over the contagion time window. Since all the uploaded calls are made unlinkable to each other, thanks to the blindness of the signature scheme and the use of anonymous channels, even if Adv is the recipient of certain calls, Adv is in general unable to link all the calls generated by the same user U. Obviously, there are some inherent leaks in extreme situations like when there is only one new infected person in the area where pseudonyms have been collected by the adversary. Such leaks are seemingly inherent and Pronto-C2 provides the strong resilience against shameless tracing.

Bombolo attack: Adv consists of Server and HA colluding together. When users are tested positive, they upload data to the system. Adv uses such data to compute additional information about infected users beyond the data they reported, such as the number of their contacts and co-location information among other infected users.
Pronto-C2 is vulnerable to this attack. Indeed, the number of calls to AuthService sent by U is clearly exposed. We note that this leak of information can be mitigated through dummy calls. It is important to note that co-location information among infected users is not leaked since two infected users who met each other will upload uncorrelated data.

Brutus attack: this attack allows Adv to link the pseudonyms of a user with his real identity. Adv is colluding with the server and the health authorities and tries to discover the real identity of the users uploading data to the server.
This attack fails with Pronto-C2. The data uploaded by a user U in Pronto-C2 cannot be linked to the real identity of U. Data are uploaded in the following steps:

1) when the infected user interacts with AuthService in order to obtain the blind signatures of the calls, and
2) when the infected user uploads the calls to Server along with the unblinded signatures.

The first step involves uploading the authorization code Code to AuthService in order to obtain the blind signature of the calls. Since HA knows the real identity of each infected user, it is possible for Adv to link the blind signature requests with an infected person. However, since the upload of the calls is performed through an anonymous channel, Adv cannot link the calls with the signature requests thanks to the blindness property of the signature scheme. This of course hides the identity behind the uploaded data only inside the set of the infected users, which is known to Adv.

Gossip attack: Adv has the same capability as a regular user of the system. The attack is successful if Adv can produce plausible digital evidence of an encounter with an infected user. The lack of resilience to the Gossip attack can be also seen as a potential feature since overwhelmed laboratories could prioritize requests for tests of citizens who can present a reasonable proof of contact with an infected user. At first sight, one could think that a proof of contact with an infected user U can be given by user providing a proof about the calls on the bulletin board. For instance, let A be a user holding a secret key sk_A corresponding to Eph_A and let Eph_U be the ephemeral key of a user U. If A finds a call $K = H(\mathsf{Eph}_\mathsf{U}^{\mathsf{sk}_\mathsf{A}}||\mathsf{Eph}_\mathsf{U}||\mathsf{Eph}_\mathsf{A})$ on the bulletin board, A could prove that he knows the secret key sk_A corresponding to Eph_A and that K is computed as before, thus proving that U made a call to A. However, in Pronto-C2, all the pseudonyms used by the users are made public on the bulletin board. So, even if A was never in contact with U, A could use Eph_U, that is public on the bulletin board, to compute a call $K = H(\mathsf{Eph}_\mathsf{U}^{\mathsf{sk}_\mathsf{A}}||\mathsf{Eph}_\mathsf{U}||\mathsf{Eph}_\mathsf{A})$ (a call from U to A) and show sk_A as proof of the fact that such call has been done. Generally, any proof of the fact that U made a call to A is *not* evidence of the fact that U met A since such proof could have been computed by A even if U was never in contact with A. Notice, however, that in the case A is not infected, what we have just described is instead plausible evidence of the fact that U met A: indeed, only infected users can write calls to the bulletin board and U is honest (if U is dishonest, the pair U and A can be seen as a single adversary). For this reason, we say that the attack affects Pronto-C2 minimally in the sense that an attacker A can provide a proof (that, as shown before, is the secret key sk_A) of the contact between U and A that convinces a third party B who believes that A is not infected.

Matteotti attack: Adv attempts to produce false alerts by causing non-at-risk users to get notified of a risk. The adversary can collude with the server and the health authorities and place passive BLE devices at locations of his choice.
This attack is not applicable to Pronto-C2. Every call K stored

Attacks	Low-cost DP-3T	Unlinkable DP-3T	Pronto-C2
Paparazzi	✗	✓	✓
Orwell	✗	✗	✓
Matrix	✗	✗	✓
Bombolo	✓	✓	✛
Brutus	✗	✗	✓
Gossip	✗	✗	✛
Matteotti	✓	✗	✓
Replay	✗	✓	✓

Figure 1. Identified attacks. We show which system is susceptible to which attack. ✗ denotes that the system is vulnerable to the attack, ✓ safety against the attack and ✛ minimal impact from the attack.

on the bulletin board has the form $K = H(K'||\mathsf{Eph}_\mathsf{C}||\mathsf{Eph}_\mathsf{B})$. A user B who at some time t broadcasts Eph_B will be notified a risk only if B received at time t an ephemeral key Eph_C and $K' = \mathsf{Eph}_\mathsf{C}^{\mathsf{sk}_\mathsf{B}}$. Since it is hard for Adv to compute K' without knowing sk_B or sk_C, we conclude that B is alerted only when B actually met C and C put an alert for B. However, in such case the alert corresponds to an actual risk for B and does not represent a successful attack.

Replay attack: Adv collects pseudonyms at a location X where the probability to meet an infected person is high and broadcasts such pseudonyms to users at a different location Y. The listened pseudonyms are broadcast at a later time slot. This attack is not applicable to Pronto-C2. An adversary Adv who broadcasts, at location X, the pseudonym of a user U_1 collected during a prior time slot in a different location Y, would fail in the attempt of causing false at-risk notifications. Indeed, to be notified, a user U_2 needs to find, on the bulletin board, a call which is directed to himself and is generated by the infected user U_1. Since the generation of such call requires the secret key of U_1 related to the time slot when the alleged meeting took place, it would be computationally infeasible for Adv to trigger a fake at-risk notification for U_2. In Figure 1 we compare Pronto-C2 with DP-3T in relation to the above attacks. The second column of the table refers to a protocol proposed by the DP-3T team in which the server computes a Cuckoo filter containing the pseudonyms of the infected users.

Acknowledgments

The full version of this paper can be found on ePrint [3].

This research has been supported in part by the European Union's Horizon 2020 research and innovation programme under grant agreement No 780477 (project PRIViLEDGE), by region Campania (POR) and by national funds (PON).

References

[1] "TraceTogether - behind the scenes look at its development process," https://www.tech.gov.sg/media/technews/tracetogether-behind-the-scenes-look-at-its-development-process.

[2] Apple and Google, "Privacy-Preserving Contact Tracing," *https://www.apple.com/covid19/contacttracing*.

[3] G. Avitabile, V. Botta, V. Iovino, and I. Visconti, "Towards defeating mass surveillance and SARS-CoV-2: The Pronto-C2 fully decentralized automatic contact tracing system," IACR ePrint Arch., Report 2020/493, 2020, https://eprint.iacr.org/2020/493.

[4] G. Avitabile, D. Friolo, and I. Visconti, "TEnK-U: Terrorist attacks for fake exposure notifications in contact tracing systems," IACR ePrint Arch., Report 2020/1150, 2020, https://eprint.iacr.org/2020/1150.

[5] L. Baumgärtner, A. Dmitrienko, B. Freisleben, J. Höchst, M. Mezini, M. Miettinen, T. D. Nguyen, A. Penning, F. Roos, A.-R. Sadeghi, M. Schwarz, and C. Uhl, "Mind the GAP: Security & privacy risks of contact tracing apps," in *TrustCom 2020, Security Track*, 2020, pp. 458–467.

[6] M. Bellare, C. Namprempre, D. Pointcheval, and M. Semanko, "The one-more-rsa-inversion problems and the security of chaum's blind signature scheme," *J. Cryptol.*, vol. 16, no. 3, pp. 185–215, 2003.

[7] F. Buccafurri, V. D. Angelis, and C. Labrini, "A privacy-preserving solution for proximity tracing avoiding identifier exchanging," in *Proc. of International Conference on Cyberworlds*. IEEE, 2020, pp. 235–242.

[8] R. Canetti, Y. T. Kalai, A. Lysyanskaya, R. L. Rivest, A. Shamir, E. Shen, A. Trachtenberg, M. Varia, and D. J. Weitzner, "Privacy-preserving automated exposure notification," IACR ePrint Arch., Report 2020/863, 2020, https://eprint.iacr.org/2020/863.

[9] A. D. Carli, M. F. Franco, A. Gassmann, C. Killer, B. Rodrigues, E. J. Scheid, D. Schoenbaechler, and B. Stiller, "Wetrace - A privacy-preserving mobile COVID-19 tracing approach and application," *CoRR*, vol. abs/2004.08812, 2020.

[10] J. Chan, L. P. Cox, D. P. Foster, S. Gollakota, E. Horvitz, J. Jaeger, S. M. Kakade, T. Kohno, J. Langford, J. Larson, P. Sharma, S. Singanamalla, J. E. Sunshine, and S. Tessaro, "PACT: privacy-sensitive protocols and mechanisms for mobile contact tracing," *IEEE Data Eng. Bull.*, vol. 43, no. 2, pp. 15–35, 2020.

[11] DP-3T's Team, "Decentralized Privacy-Preserving Proximity Tracing," *https://github.com/DP-3T/documents/blob/master/DP3T%20White%20Paper.pdf*.

[12] DP-3T's Team, "Response to Analysis of DP3T: Between Scylla and Charybdis," https://github.com/DP-3T/documents/blob/master/Security%20analysis/Response%20to%20'Analysis%20of%20DP3T'.pdf.

[13] L. Ferretti, C. Wymant, M. Kendall, L. Zhao, A. Nurtay, L. Abeler-Dörner, M. Parker, D. Bonsall, and C. Fraser, "Quantifying sars-cov-2 transmission suggests epidemic control with digital contact tracing," *Science*, vol. 368, no. 6491, 2020.

[14] Fraunhofer AISEC, "Pandemic contact tracing apps: Dp-3t, pepp-pt ntk, and robert from a privacy perspective," IACR ePrint Arch., Report 2020/489, 2020, https://eprint.iacr.org/2020/489.

[15] Inria PRIVATICS Team, "DESIRE: A Third Way for a European Exposure Notification System," https://github.com/3rd-ways-for-EU-exposure-notification/project-DESIRE/blob/master/DESIRE-specification-EN-v1_0.pdf, 2020.

[16] Inria PRIVATICS Team, "ROBERT: ROBust and privacy-presERving proximity Tracing," https://github.com/ROBERT-proximity-tracing/documents/blob/master/ROBERT-specification-EN-v1_0.pdf, 2020.

[17] PACT's Team, "Decentralized privacy-preserving proximity tracing," *https://pact.mit.edu/wp-content/uploads/2020/04/The-PACT-protocol-specification-ver-0.1.pdf*, 2020.

[18] K. Pietrzak, "Delayed authentication: Preventing replay and relay attacks in private contact tracing," in *Proc. of Progress in Cryptology - INDOCRYPT 2020 - Lecture Notes in Computer Science*, vol. 12578. Springer, 2020, pp. 3–15.

[19] B. Pinkas and E. Ronen, "Hashomer - a proposal for a privacy-preserving bluetooth based contact tracing scheme for Hamagen," https://github.com/eyalr0/HashomerCryptoRef/blob/master/documents/hashomer.pdf, 2020.

[20] O. Seiskari, "Contact Tracing BLE sniffer PoC," https://github.com/oseiskari/corona-sniffer, 2020.

[21] Q. Tang, "Privacy-preserving contact tracing: current solutions and open questions," *CoRR*, vol. abs/2004.06818, 2020.

[22] TCNCoalition, "TCN Protocol," https://github.com/TCNCoalition/TCN#the-tcn-protocol, 2020.

[23] S. Vaudenay, "Analysis of DP3T," IACR ePrint Arch., Report 2020/399, 2020, https://eprint.iacr.org/2020/399.

[24] S. Vaudenay, "Centralized or decentralized? The contact tracing dilemma," IACR ePrint Arch., Report 2020/531, 2020, https://eprint.iacr.org/2020/531.